Perfecting Moments
Empowering God's Kingdom One Thought at a Time
Dr. Theresa Scott

I0083404

Copyright © 2019 by Dr. Theresa Scott
Published by Pecan Tree Publishing

Unless otherwise noted, all Scripture quotations are from the King James Version of the Bible.

Scripture quotations marked AMP are taken from THE AMPLIFIED BIBLE, Old Testament copyright © 1965, 1987 by the Zondervan Corporation. The Amplified New Testament copyright © 1958, 1987 by The Lockman Foundation. Used by permission.

Scripture quotations marked NIV are taken from the HOLY BIBLE, NEW INTERNATIONAL VERSION ®. Copyright © 1973, 1978, 1984 by International Bible Society. Used by permission of Zondervan Publishing House. All rights reserved.

Scripture quotations marked NLT are taken from the *Holy Bible*, New Living Translation, copyright © 1996, 2004, 2007 by Tyndale House Foundation. Used by permission of Tyndale House Publishers, Inc., Carol Stream, Illinois 60188. All rights reserved.

Scripture quotations marked MSG are taken from THE MESSAGE. Copyright © 1993, 1994, 1995. Used by permission of NavPress Publishing Group.

978-1-7347430-0-5 Paperback
978-1-7347430-1-2 Digital
Library of Congress Catalog Number: 2020904600

Cover and Interior Design by: Charlyn Samson

Author Photo Credit:
Jonothan Dashiell
JAK Visual Arts
www.jonmichal.com
info@jonmichal.com

Pecan Tree Publishing
www.pecantreebooks.com

New Voices | New Styles | New Vision –
Creating a New Legacy of Dynamic Authors and Titles
Hollywood, FL

CONTENTS

Perfecting MOMENTS

EMPOWERING
God's Kingdom
ONE THOUGHT AT A TIME

DR. THERESA SCOTT

ACKNOWLEDGEMENTS

I want to thank God for leading me on this journey of broadcasting Perfecting Moments eight years ago. I am grateful for the staff and listeners of 90.3 WDIH Radio (Salisbury, MD) who encouraged me during those years.

I am most grateful for my church family at Grow in Grace Worship Center, Delmar, MD, for their prayers of intercession and encouragement.

More importantly, I thank God for my husband (Bishop Richard Scott) who supports me in every endeavor I take on. He is my Earth Angel. I thank my children (Jason and Amira), and my grandson (Jordan) for believing in me and pushing me to leave this legacy book in the earth.

FOREWORD

Perfecting Moments embodies Philippians 3:12 – *"Not as though I had already attained, either were already perfect: but I follow after, if that I may apprehend that for which also I am apprehended of Christ Jesus."*

The words are spiritual wisdom mandating a search of ourselves for the Straight Path which will allow us to walk therein, just as the Scripture declares to us. *Perfecting Moments* allow us to take an introspective look at the man/woman in the mirror and when we do each day, we will come to grips with profound challenges and even encouraging moments all wrapped up in what is known as *Moments* of perfection.

Over the years, *Perfecting Moments* aired on 90.3 FM WDIH Radio, where I work. These *Moments* were times where you just had to ponder and reflect on their beauty – words to indeed perfect one's life. I believe you'll be enlightened and strengthened by what you are about to encounter.

A better you is on the way all because Dr. Theresa Scott has mastered a way to see self in the Light. Her messages declare that we are indeed a work in progress, a people who have not arrived, but are arriving. Like clay in the hands of the Potter, *Perfecting Moments* will sear and grind you spiritually. When it's all done, it produces pure gold in you. Now it is time to allow the *Moments* you are about to experience lead to a greater you.

Bill Lee
Marketing Consultant
90.3 FM WDIH Radio

9

INTRODUCTION

The Bible tells us that a word spoken in due season is good! (Proverbs 15:23) Sometimes all we need is a timely word from God through His vessels to soothe our hearts, calm our fears and encourage our spirit. Life is too short to dwell on negativity when there is so much life in Christ. *"I came that they may have and enjoy life, and have it in abundance (to the full, till it overflows)."* (John 10:10, AMP) The pressures of life can be overwhelming to the point of stressing us out. Yet during those times, God sends us words of comfort and encouragement like a cool breeze on a summer day.

Perfecting Moments is a compilation of one-minute radio broadcasts I did over an eight-year span. During that time the radio broadcast received two awards - 2012 WDIH 90.3 FM Program of the Year Award and Broadcast Ministry Award, (www.wdihradio90-3.org). *Perfecting Moments* proved to be a daily compass for the believers' walk in Christ.

The purpose of the segment was to challenge and inspire the Body of Christ to greater spiritual and personal development. Ephesians 4:12 tells us that Jesus gave gifts to the Body of Christ to **perfect** them. That perfecting means to bring them to a place of maturity. To grow us up to reflect a genuine life in Christ. These *Perfecting Moments* are thought provoking – causing one to examine themselves in all areas of life. They are also sources of encouragement – nudging us along during life's adversities.

It is my prayer that your life will be enhanced as you read and meditate on these ***Perfecting Moments*** designed especially with you in mind.

Dr. Theresa Scott
Email: lgcebks@gmail.com
Facebook: Theresa Scott
Instagram: Dr. Theresa Scott

Perfecting
DECISIONS

NEED WISDOM

Sometimes it's hard to make a quality decision during chaos and confusion. God knew it when He said, *"if any man lacks wisdom let him ask and He will give it liberally."* (James 1:5) If you are in the process of making a major decision, I encourage you to be thorough and led by God to get you through the maze of confusion and chaos into victory. Be deliberate in your decision making by choosing righteousness, peace and joy. Pay attention to the checks in your spirit that require you to stop before you make a mistake in judgment or put yourself in harm's way.

CONSEQUENCES

Don't spend another stressful day trying to make a crucial decision. You have the Holy Spirit as your Guide. He speaks in a still small voice. Hear Him in stillness. Exercise your discernment in your pursuit to know what is real and good. Learn the difference between treasure and junk – spiritually and naturally. Otherwise you will find yourself distracted from the path of God's will for your life. Consider the consequences both long-term and short-term. Pay attention. Stay the course. *"In all thy ways acknowledge Him, and He shall direct thy paths."* (Proverbs 3:6)

MISTAKES

Don't allow the urgency of a situation to cause you to make a wrong decision. Pressured urgency comes from your adversary. He doesn't want you to think things through. There are times when prolonged thinking must cease, and a decision made. Even in that, seek the peace and wisdom of God. Remember God is never in a hurry. No matter what you decide it will be a leap of faith because without faith you can't please God. Don't get stuck in making a mistake. Mistakes are not the end of the world. They teach you what didn't work. It should push you to pursue what does work.

PERSONAL POWER

Did you know decision making is a powerful force in your life? Think about it. Decision making involves methodical thinking. You weigh the positives and the negatives. You engage in mental scenarios concerning an issue or situation. The dictionary defines *decide* as bringing or coming to a resolution in favor of one side or another. You reach a conclusion in decision making. You resolve to do or not to do. That power resides in you. *"Every passing moment is another chance to turn your life around."* (Cameron Crowe, Writer) Decide how you want your life to be. Exercise your personal power.

MAKE UP YOUR MIND

Do you feel like you're stuck in life? Does it seem as if life is passing you by? Is everything around you progressing, moving and changing? I know your life is in God's hands, but your life is in your hands as well. God gives you life, but you must live it. Second Peter 1:3 says God *"has given us all things that pertain to life and godliness."* There is absolutely no reason for you to be unproductive and stuck in life. If you are, that's a choice you have made. You can't blame anyone for where you are in life right now. *"The first step toward getting somewhere is to decide that you are not going to stay where you are."* (J. P. Morgan, Financier and Banker)

DESTINY CHOICES

Your choices form your life. The decisions you make now affect your future. Your future involves your destiny. Therefore, your choices need to be well thought out. Are your choices in line with God's will for you? Don't just live for the moment and make hasty decisions. Choices have consequences – good or bad. When you make choices according to your goals and dreams, it keeps you in line with your destiny. *"Destiny is not a matter of chance, it is a matter of choice; it is not a thing to be waited for, it is a thing to be achieved."* (William Jennings Bryan, Orator and Politician)

VALLEY OF DECISION

If you're in a valley of decision this might encourage you. Think before you act. Consider the consequences. Your decision will not only affect you but others as well. Take into consideration the long-term effects – don't just live for the moment. I'm not trying to get you outside of the realm of faith, but faith should be accompanied with wise counsel. Get the counsel. Just remember the final decision is on you. Don't allow the urgency of a matter to force you into something you will regret later. Be still and hear God. Your decision will have future consequences. *"It is in your moments of decision that your destiny is shaped."* (Tony Robbins, Author and Philanthropist) Keep your decision within the boundaries of your destiny.

MAN UP!

Far too often we blame our plight in life on past experiences or other people. We hide behind being overlooked, discriminated upon, inequalities, and so on. We tend to relish in what we feel was not provided for us. We give discrimination, prejudice and inequality too much power. We allow it to determine the course of our lives. I believe we do this because we don't want to be responsible. You were created with a will and a mind to pick and choose at your own discretion. From the *Narrative of the Life of Frederick Douglass* written in 1845, Mr. Douglass, Abolitionist and Statesman, put it like this – ***"You have seen how a man was made a slave; you shall see how a slave was made a man."*** It's time for you to *man up*!

FREEDOM

Harriet Tubman, Abolitionist and Political Activist once said ***"When I found I had crossed that line, [on her first escape from slavery, 1845] I looked at my hands to see if I was the same person. There was such a glory over everything."*** This is what you experience when you take that step of faith away from the people and situations that have you bound. You quickly discover freedom is really a glorious thing. I don't know what has limited you or held you captive, but it's time to move from that place and step into the liberty Christ has provided for you. ***"If the Son therefore shall make you free, ye shall be free indeed."*** (John 8:36)

YOUR WILL

All of us have a free will. Even God won't violate your will. Your will is something you have power over. Our will is governed by our choices. We choose what we will and will not do. This is one of the reasons our walk with Christ is relational and not religious. ***"Love the Lord your God with all your heart and with all your soul and with all your mind."*** (Matthew 22:37) This is an act of your will. It's a choice. We have many liberties as a Christian but must realize ***"Everything is permissible, but not everything is beneficial. Everything is permissible, but not everything is construc-***

tive. "(First Corinthians 10:23, NIV) Orchestrate your life into what is constructive for your Christian welfare.

PUT OFF AND PUT ON

How many times have you gotten stuck trying to figure out what to wear? I go through this more than I need to – putting on something and then taking it off because the outfit didn't come together. The issue is making a decision. God leaves us with decisions to put off and put on things in our lives. This is our responsibility. Ephesians 4:17-29 tells us to *put off* the old man and *put on* the new man. You have the capability to do this. Everyday decide to *put away the old* way of living that corrupts your new nature and decide to *put on a new* mindset and lifestyle that reflects righteousness and true holiness.

HOW TO PUT OFF AND PUT ON

How do you *put off* the habits of the old man and put on the habits of a new man? First get to know Christ – study Him through the scriptures. The Word of God tells you what's required of you, but always remember you're not alone in accomplishing this. You have the Holy Spirit to help you. He is with you to **"conform you into the image of Christ Jesus."** (Romans 8:29) Remember the Holy Spirit helps you *to do.* You initiate it and He will help you execute it. Just make up your mind *to do it.*

REACTIONS

In reflecting over my life, I can agree with a statement Chuck Swindoll, Pastor and Author, made, **"life is 10% what happens to you and 90% how you react to it."** I've experienced the good and the bad. My reaction to the good was a no-brainer. But the bad sometimes got me in trouble. God allows the good and the bad in our lives. Yet it's how we react to them that reveals our level of maturity. As life continues to bring me good and bad, it shows me myself. After seasons of good and bad I didn't like what I saw, so I changed how I reacted. Little by little God shows us ourselves. He then says in a small still voice – *"see it another way."*

SUCCESSFUL DISCIPLINES

Everybody wants to be successful. We read books. We study the lives of successful people. Great sums of money are spent just to be in the presence of successful people. We do all these things in hopes of finding their secrets to success. Well, success comes in different ways. We tend to attribute success to financial and materialistic gain. I believe before success is manifested in that manner, there must first be inward success. ***"Success is nothing more than a few simple disciplines, practiced every day."*** (Jim Rohn, Entrepreneur and Author) Discipline and success go hand in hand. Discipline involves consistency – consistency in godliness, integrity, being trustworthy, honest, truthful, reliable, considerate, dependable, etc. This should be practiced every day.

Perfecting
DISTRACTIONS

STAY PLANTED

There is a quote that says, ***"The tallest oak in the forest was once just a little nut that held its ground."*** (Unknown) This led me to think how a forest comes into being. Actually no one plants a forest. It grows on its own by the seeds that fall to the ground and remain there nurtured by the rain and sun. Once that seed is in the ground it stays there. It grows at its own pace and endures the seasons of nature. If it stays in its place, it develops a deep root system. What's the point here? Stay where you're planted. God planted you in Him - stay there. He planted you in the Holy Spirit - stay there. He planted you in faith – stay there. He planted you in a ministry – stay there. Don't uproot yourself – stay and grow!!

DECEPTIONS

Deuteronomy 8:19, NIV says ***"And if you ever forget the Lord your God and follow other gods and worship and bow down to them, I testify against you today that you will surely be destroyed."*** King James Version says ***"ye shall surely perish."*** The god of this world has orchestrated things to move you away from all that represents God. He is a shrewd god. If you aren't careful to keep a check on yourself and your relationship with Christ, you can be drawn away. In and of yourself, you are no match for the god of this world. It takes the power of the Holy Spirit and your commitment to stay connected to God. Eve got drawn away when Satan told her God didn't really mean what He said. She didn't die naturally, but spiritually. Little by little you die spiritually. You lose ground in your relationship with God when you slack off and become disobedient.

PIED PIPER OF LIFE 1

Each day, week, month and year offers you an opportunity to fulfill purpose in life. You can become so accustomed to distractions that you lose sight of yourself. Responsibilities surround you to the point it tempts you into thinking they are the most important things of your life. If you aren't careful, they will take over and you will spend your life serving them. Don't fall under the spell of the **Pied Piper of Life**. He cleverly draws you away from destiny. He will put you to sleep. He will cause you to forget who you really are and why you are here. Wake up!

PIED PIPER OF LIFE 2

The **Pied Piper of Life** plays a tune we're all familiar with. It's the tune that cleverly draws us away from ourselves. His music is spell binding. His aim is to get you to fall asleep at the wheel of your life. The **Pied Piper of Life** draws you away from the path you were meant to follow. One way to overcome his power is to rekindle your passion. Think about how you can make a difference. Don't get drawn under his spell of procrastination living only for a weekend or holiday, or ritually watching TV all the time. This causes you to become oblivious to who you are and what you possess. There is a reason for your existence.

PIED PIPER OF LIFE 3

There's a saying that *"if you keep doing the same thing, you will get the same results."* To get different results you've got to do something different. If you've fallen under the spell of the **Pied Piper of Life** and keep dancing to his music, things will never change. Try this – entertain positive/productive thoughts, emotions or actions. This sets up a chain of events that takes your life in a different direction. Each positive action you take replaces a mindless action. You slowly replace the tune of the **Pied Piper of Life** with your own sound of thoughts and actions. Eventually you will become the **Pied Piper of Your Own Life** and follow the music of the authentic life you were meant to live.

DREAMS

Have you ever dreamed about how you want your life to be? I'm talking about seeing yourself fulfilling your passion. I'm sure your dreams seem almost impossible, but they are achievable. These dreams are the callings of your heart. Let me ask you this – *do your dreams have you or do you have your dreams?* Dreams are part of your subconscious. There is a part of you that is longing to come to the forefront of your life. Give credence to your dreams. They are possible. Start acting upon them. It's your life.

Perfecting
ENCOURAGEMENT

POWER OF ENCOURAGEMENT

Encouragement is a powerful force. Think about all the times someone encouraged you and how it kept you going. When we encourage each other, it brings clarity to our lives. Encouragement keeps you on the right path. Encouragement says *yes* when everything else says *no*. Encouragement builds you up. Encouragement lets you know someone really cares. Encouragement keeps you believing in yourself. Encouragement pushes you past your dilemma. Encouragement lifts your spirit. I could go on and on. But I want to encourage you to make it a point to encourage somebody. What you say or do will make their day. Finally, *"encouragement helps people to change their story."* (Michael McKinney, Author) I almost didn't write this book, but Michael told me someone is waiting to read it. Thanks for the encouragement. Who is waiting for your encouraging word?

ENCOURAGE YOURSELF

One of the most powerful things human beings can do for one another is to say something encouraging, complimentary or positive. We live in such a negative world; so, anything positive is like a breath of fresh air. We value words of empowerment from others. It strengthens our esteem. What happens when we don't get the compliments or encouragement? Well, we have the power of life or death in our mouths. What can you say to yourself to nurture your esteem and affirm your worth? *"At the end of the day, tell yourself gently: 'I love you, you did the best you could today, and even if you didn't accomplish all you had planned, I love you anyway.'"* (Francois, Author) Learn how to affirm who you are and encourage yourself.

SHAKE IT OFF

The Apostle Paul was well acquainted with adversities and afflictions. He suffered many things for the sake of Christ. God did not withhold suffering from him, so Paul had to learn how to manage it. (Philippians 4:11-12) He had to change his perspective about suffering. He noticed that at his weakest times, the power of Christ was more prominent. (Second Corinthians 12:10) Paul was shipwrecked and landed on the island of Melita. While gathering some wood for the fire, a snake bit him. Paul didn't panic. He shook the snake off. (Acts 28:3-5) That snake bite was nothing compared to all he had gone through. God is working on you via trials and tribulations to get you to the point where you won't panic in the midst of them, but just shake it off.

DO IT ANYWAY

Your heartfelt dreams and aspirations should not be ignored. God placed a passion in each of us to help others and make a difference in the world. What's important to you may not be important to someone else. Go with what's in your heart. It's in your heart, not someone else's. Stop waiting for others to see what only you can see. Don't deprive the world of what's in you. Pursue it. *"It's impossible said pride. It's risky said experience. It's pointless said reason. Give it a try whispered the heart."* (Unknown)

TAKE A STEP

"If you do not step forward, you'll always be in the same place." (Nora Roberts, Author) That's a thought-provoking statement. It led me to the scripture that says, *"faith without works is dead."* (James 2:20) The statement and scripture speak of the same thing — *movement* and *action*. I have a way of entertaining various scenarios to pursue what I need to do. I see myself in it and doing it, but it's only in my mind. I'm just exercising mental energy. Thinking is not doing. Doing is doing. If I'm serious about what I want, I must take deliberate actions and move in the direction I need to go in. Take a step!

KEEP DOING GOOD

The Bible admonishes us not to get weary in well-doing. (Galatians 6:9) Don't lose heart or get tired in doing what's right. We start out well and somewhere down the road we fall by the wayside. We get distracted and discouraged. We don't get appreciated like we think we should and are often taken for granted. In addition, we have an adversary who will do anything he can to stop us from doing good. I want to encourage you to continue to do good anyway. It will pay off in the end. Keep doing good so things will go well in your life. Remember God is taking note of your works and motives. What will be read in your Book of Life? (Revelations 20:12)

YOU ARE OKAY

Are you okay with *you*? I mean do you have a good relationship with *you*? I know these questions sound crazy. Do you like *you*? When we look at ourselves, we tend to focus on the negative - what is *wrong*. Yet there are things that are *right*. This doesn't mean having a haughty or superior estimation on yourself. There are some things that are quite *right* with you. Hang out with yourself and speak life to the positive areas in your life. Start keeping company with *you*. Speak *good* things to *you*. ***"You cannot be lonely if you like the person you're alone with."*** (Wayne Dyer, Author) You are alone with *you* 24-7.

OPEN DOOR

Alexander Graham Bell, Inventor, once said, ***"When one door closes, another opens; but we often look so long and so regretfully upon the closed door that we do not see the one which has opened for us."*** Is this you? Stop having memorial services for things that were shut down, didn't work, and left you in a pitiful state. That's all a part of life. The door closed. Turn around. Look at the open door. The open door is a new opportunity, second chance, new beginning. An open door brings new adventure, challenges for you to explore, discover greater things about yourself and your God. For every closed door there is an open door.

DON'T QUIT

Don't let the cares of life beat you down. I know you're tired, but don't *quit*. Take a break. Soak in the tub. Sit on a bench in the park. Drive your car near a nice water spot. Look up at the sky – gaze upon the clouds and stars. Embrace a cool breeze. Whatever you do, don't *quit*. Tell God all about it. Cast all your cares on Him because He cares, but don't *quit*. Cry if you must, scream as loud as you can, but don't *quit*. Inhale and exhale. Push your car seat back and close your eyes, but don't *quit*. ***"Once you learn to quit, it becomes a habit."*** (Vince Lombardi, Football Player and Coach) You've got an inner strength in you that whispers *"You can do this thing called living!"*

RESTORATION

One of God's greatest joys is to bring restoration to the lives of His people. Psalm 23:3 says *"He restoreth my soul."* Joel 2:25 says *"I will restore to you the years that the locust hath eaten, the cankerworm, and the caterpillar, and the palmerworm."* To receive restoration, you need to know what was taken – what you lost. These locusts were swarming, crawling, consuming, and chewing locusts. God identified what they lost. Then He said He would restore. What have you lost? How can you be restored when you don't know what you lost? Did you lose good health? Suffer a financial loss? Fired from a job? Missed an opportunity? Identify what you lost so God can bring restoration to your life. Allow Him to heal you inwardly - your spirit and soul. Then you can more readily receive the external restoration in the way He wants to do it.

IT'S WORTH IT

I want to encourage you in your walk with Christ by letting you know it's worth serving and living for Him. Keep the faith even when life comes at you hard. Fulfill your purpose on earth so you can receive your crown. (Revelations 3:11) *"Let us fix our eyes on Jesus, the author and perfecter of our faith, who for the joy set before him endured the cross, scorning its shame, and sat down at the right hand of the throne of God. Consider him who endured such opposition from sinful men, so that you will not grow weary and lose heart."* (Hebrews 12:2-3)

HEAVEN'S REWARD

There are benefits and rewards for keeping a heavenly focus. Your focus should be doing the will of God to ensure you receive a just reward in heaven. How you finish is vital. That's why the journey must be intentional. Jesus is our example. He knew His goal was to die on the cross, rise from the grave, and be seated at the right hand of God for our sake. It was Jesus' journey that strengthens our faith. He endured persecution and shame. Despite everything He went through, He kept going in and towards His purpose. His reward was heaven and so is yours. Keep the faith!

DETERMINATION

Have you ever made up your mind to do something then suddenly every distraction known comes your way? It's crazy, but it's true. What do you do? Do you quit, give up or what? Well, it all depends on how important it is to you. Break the habit of altering your plans or goals because of distractions and other people's agenda. Don't allow timely opportunities to pass you by. *"Construct your determination with Sustained Effort, Controlled Attention, and Concentrated Energy. Opportunities never come to those who wait – they are captured by those who dare to attack."* (Paul J. Meyer, Entrepreneur and Author)

WILLPOWER

I read a proverb that said, *"When the will is ready the feet are light."* (Unknown) That's willpower. Willpower is a made-up mind to do something. Every endeavor, task, or assignment starts with a thought. After you methodically think it through, the next step is an act of your will. This is when you determine to do it. Your mind is made up. There is no room for dissuasion. You may be considering doing something you've given a lot of thought to. Let me encourage you to take action and *do it*. Get it out of your head and manifest it. We've been waiting for it!

OBSTACLES

Henry Ford, Industrialist, once said, *"Obstacles are those frightful things you see when you take your eyes off your goal."* So, my friend, what obstacle are you facing that is preventing you from reaching your goal? Is it fear, failure, lack of resources, opinions of others or your own self-doubt? Whatever it is, it only has the power you give it. Your goal is more important than the obstacle. Work around or through the obstacle so you can achieve your goal. Persevere. Don't give up. Don't give in. Remember, you are *MORE than a conqueror.* (Romans 8:31)

TOMORROW

Tomorrow, tomorrow, tomorrow – the root cause of procrastination. We have this terrible tendency to persistently put undesirable tasks off to another day. Tomorrow is not promised to anyone. Jesus said – *"We must work the works of Him Who sent Me and be busy with His business while it is daylight; night is coming on, when no man can work."* (John 9:4) You got health and strength *today* to accomplish your task. Who knows how you will be *tomorrow?* *"Tomorrow is the only day in the year that appeals to a lazy man."* (Jimmy Lyons, Musician)

INCOMPLETE TASKS

How do you feel when you are unable to complete a task? Well, I don't know about you, but I feel like I lied to myself – like I let myself down. Think about it. First, it took you forever just thinking about it. Second, you talked yourself in and out of it. One minute you were ready, the next minute you weren't. Nevertheless, the task must still be done. Constant procrastination will stress you out. The time you spend stressing over it, you could have completed it. Finish what you start. *"Nothing is so fatiguing as the eternal hanging on of an uncompleted task."* (William James, Philosopher and Psychologist)

STAY THE COURSE

"Consider the postage stamp; its usefulness consists in the ability to stick to one thing till it gets there." (Josh Billings, Writer and Lecturer) This really encouraged me. I start things and somewhere down the line I drift away. Distractions overtake me. This encouraged me to stay the course and finish what I started. Let me encourage you to finish what you start. Even if it doesn't turn out the way you want, finish anyhow. Stick with it. Remember, it's not how you start that matters, it's that you finish what you began.

A PROMISE IS A PROMISE

When God saved us, He did not leave us to figure out how we are to live our lives in Him. He told us He would *"never leave us nor forsake us."* (Hebrews 13:5) He promised to be with us, and nothing could ever separate us from His love. (Romans 8:35, 39) He gives us promises that He keeps. He's not like man who is subject to not keeping his word. *"God is not a man that He should lie; neither the son of man that he should repent: hath he said, and shall he not do it? Or hath he spoken, and shall he not make it good?"* (Numbers 23:19) A promise is a promise. God is committed to His Word.

TOUGH TIMES

You are living in the best time of your life. Now when you read that, you probably immediately equated your life with your present circumstances. You looked at every need and lack you're challenged with. You are so focused on your crises that you can't mentally perceive any good in it. Well my friend, stop, look and listen. *"Tough times don't last, tough people do."* (Robert H. Schuller, Pastor and Author) You are stronger than you realize. You got what it takes to endure the unendurable. Take note of your strengths because you got it like that!!

DO IT AGAIN

Proverbs 24:16 says *"For a just man falleth seven times, and riseth up again...."* Falling in life is inevitable because life is trial and error. The mere fact you fell meant you were standing or moving in a direction you believed in. *"Success is getting up one more time."* (Unknown) When you fail at something one time that means there are more ways to discover success. Don't allow mistakes or failures to keep you down. Falling is one thing but staying down is something else. That's not you. Get up and do it again.

STICK IT OUT

Waiting on God reveals our faith and trust in Him. Stick it out. God will bring to pass what He promised. Hebrews 10:35-39, of The Message Bible says: *"So don't throw it all away now. You were sure of yourselves then. It's still a sure thing! But you need to stick it out, staying with God's plan so you'll be there for the promised completion. It won't be long now, he's on the way; he'll show up most any minute. But anyone who is right with me thrives on loyal trust; if he cuts and runs, I won't be very happy. But we're not quitters who lose out. Oh, no! We'll stay with it and survive, trusting all the way."*

WORTH WAITING

I know it seems like waiting for God to do what He said takes forever. Some things come to pass quicker than others. David experienced the same thing. He wrote how it was worth the wait in Psalm 40:1-3, MSG – *"I waited and waited for God. At last he looked; finally, he listened. He lifted me out of the ditch, pulled me from deep mud. He stood me up on a solid rock to make sure I wouldn't slip. He taught me how to sing the latest God-song, a praise-song to our God. More and more people are seeing this: they enter into the mystery, abandoning themselves to God."* It takes faith, trust and patience to wait on God. Rest in the fact that He knows what He's doing and when He'll do it. He's always on time – His time.

FINISHER

It's a wonderful thing to start a year or an endeavor with a new resolve, goals and plans. Starting is good, but it's finishing that counts. What have you completed? Did you stick to your plan? Did the issues of life interrupt your plans? If they did, always remember it's never too late to pick up where you left off. Your plans or goals have only been delayed. A completed plan is a wonderful thing. Just remember there's still more to do. If nothing was completed, all is not lost. Endeavor to finish what you started. Finish strong so you can start strong.

KEEP TRYING

Life is filled with trial and error. No one is given a handbook on how to live their lives. Everyone must deal with the good, bad and ugly. These are challenges that reveal what we're made of. Some of us sink, some of us swim. You can talk all day long about your life challenges, but it's how you handle them and what you learn from them that matters. Don't let the challenges of life shut you down. God placed a hidden strength in you that is only revealed in a challenge. Michael Jordan, Basketball Player, said *"I can accept failure. Everyone fails at something. But I can't accept not trying."* Keep at it, for it will be worth it in the end.

UNDYING HOPE

I've reflected on how our ancestors lived noble and honorable lives in Africa. Then suddenly were captured into slavery and systematically stripped of all self-worth. Yet in that awful state they envisioned their people being restored to honor and nobility. They refused to accept their plight. They fought for the ones coming after them. They left a legacy of hope and triumph. So how dare we live such mediocre lives when so much was given for us to thrive. Maya Angelou, American Poet and Author, said *"Bringing the gifts that my ancestors gave, I am the dream and the hope of the slave. I rise. I rise, I rise."*

WE, THE PEOPLE

On July 24, 1974 Barbara Jordan, Former Member of the Texas Senate, gave this statement before the House Committee on the Judiciary – *"'We, the people.' It is a very eloquent beginning. But when that document [the Preamble to the US Constitution] was completed on the 17th of Sept. in 1787 I was not included in that 'We, the people.' I felt somehow for many years that George Washington and Alexander Hamilton just left me out by mistake. But through the process of amendment, interpretation and court decision I have finally been included in 'We, the people.'"* You may feel ostracized, excluded or abandoned. Know - for a certainty - God is with you and you have a place of acceptance in Him. Stick with His process. He will see to it that you get what rightfully belongs to you.

CHALLENGES

You may not completely realize what God did when He created you. He wired you with everything you need to make it in life. Within you is an ability to withstand the storms of life. If you survived up to this point, realize there is a form of endurance within you. Life will continually present you with challenges. Allow the challenges to teach you something. Stop relishing in the challenge and celebrate the accomplishment – the results of the challenge. It has made you wiser and revealed a strength you didn't realize you had.

STAY THE COURSE

Today I thought about you and want to encourage you in your life with Christ. I know it can be a real challenge to be Christ-like. The only reason you are still in Christ is because you love Him. That's a good thing. Keep living according to Christian principles. I know it gets lonely at times because it's hard to explain the ways of Christ, but it's worth it. I challenge you to – *"Believe where others doubt. Work where others refuse. Save where others waste. Stay where others quit. And you will win where others lose."* (Ritu Ghatourey, Indian Author)

WEARY

There are times we become tired in doing good. We give of ourselves in helping others. We press day in and day out praying, encouraging, declaring and decreeing. Everyone comes to us for help when we need help ourselves. Well, the Bible says *"...let us not be not weary in well doing; for in due season we shall reap if we faint not."* (Galatians 6:9) I know you're tired, but I want you to *resist* that weariness and discouragement. Keep believing. Keep an intensity in all you set out to do. Shake yourself. Get your thoughts consistent with the Word of God for your life. Keep your eyes on the prize.

ENDURE TEMPTATION

James 1:12 says *"Blessed is the man that endureth temptation: for when he is tried, he shall receive the crown of life, which the Lord hath promised to them that love him."* The New International Version says, *"Blessed is the man who perseveres under trial, because when he has stood the test, he will receive the crown of life."* I want to encourage you to endure the temptation, persevere under the trial. I know it's rough, but remember you have the Holy Spirit to help you. Don't cave in or cower down. Don't walk away. Stand your ground. Past the test. Because at the end of this you will receive the crown of life.

GOOD NEWS

It seems when you listen to the news or hear something about someone, it is bad news. When I say *bad,* I'm talking about detrimental things, tragedies, calamities, loss of life, accidents, etc. It's *bad* because it was not favorable. We tend to put more emphasis on the bad than on the good. Sometimes the bad stayed bad, then other times the bad produced some good. I don't want you to get so caught up in our bad society that you lose focus on the good. Today, find something good to do and say. Spread some good news. Talk about the good in your life because good outweighs the bad. You have a body and mind which are functioning – that - is good news.

Perfecting FAITH

FULLY PERSUADED

Let's think for a moment about faith and believing. You've heard all the scriptures and revelations on faith. You've also heard about the levels of faith from little to great. You also understand Christians are people of faith. The scripture we gravitate to the most is *"the just shall live by faith."* (Romans 1:17; Galatians 3:11) Faith is a strong confidence in someone or something to do what is said. God has proven Himself faithful to all of us. The question now is do we believe Him. Are we fully convinced that He will do what He said? *"We believe what we tell ourselves."* (Doe Zantamata, Author) What are you telling yourself?

BELIEVE

People of God have a way of quoting scriptures but not believing scriptures. We decree and declare God's Word over our lives with little faith coupled with it. Somehow, we think God's Word is magic – just speak it and everything changes. Not so. The majority of people Jesus healed were those who believed. On numerous occasions He said their faith made them whole. He did not lay hands on many of them. He merely challenged their belief. Could there be a slight possibility that the Word of God you have been quoting has not come to pass because of unbelief? Are you really believing the scriptures? Believe in the Word a little bit more and it might just come to pass!

BREAKING THE HABIT

I don't know about you, but God has a way of getting me to break some old habits. He has allowed some things to come up in my life that changed my routine, perceptions, theories, personal doctrines, etc. He changed it for the better. I heard it takes 21 days to break a habit – three weeks. That's not long if you stick with it. Change is inevitable. You must take on a new mindset partnered with greater faith and expectation from God. If you don't start believing for the better, it will never happen. Remember *"without faith it is impossible to please him: for he that cometh to God must believe that he is, and that he is a rewarder of them that diligently seek Him."* (Hebrews 11:6)

SOLID FAITH

For far too long the Body of Christ, as many membered as it is, has a reputation of demonstrating more of its weaknesses than its strengths. The Body of Christ sadly has a track record of sending mixed signals to a dying world by saying one thing yet living something else. Don't lose your values based on what others think of you. Don't compromise your faith at the risk of being politically correct. Don't be *"ashamed of the gospel of Christ: for it is the power of God unto salvation to everyone that believeth."* (Romans 1:16) Live what you believe.

CHALLENGED FAITH

The Bible is one of the truest and most profound books in the world. It contains written words inspired by God. God inspired Paul to write to Timothy to tell him to *"fight the good fight of faith."* (First Timothy 6:12) He knew Timothy would be tremendously challenged in his faith. We are challenged every day in ours. It is a literal fight. The fight we face is the fear of *"what if"* God won't do what He said. We start with strong faith, but after a period *"what if"* shows up. *"What if"* has to be fought with *"I choose to believe God no matter what, no matter how long."* Keep believing. Keep fighting.

GOD HAS FAITH IN YOU

The Scriptures tells us far more times than we realize that we are to *"have faith in God."* (Mark 11:22) This is a requirement for the people of God because we know that *"without faith it is impossible to please Him."* (Hebrews 11:6) *Faith* is a strong and convincing belief or persuasion in some thing or someone. We believe God because He has proved Himself faithful in our lives. But can God have faith in us to trust Him – believe He will do what He said? Can He trust you to keep the faith? *"Have faith in God; God has faith in you."* (Edwin Louis Cole, Author)

FAITH ACTIVATION

God takes delight and moves on our behalf when we have faith in Him. Faith is trusting in and relying on God. Faith is knowing God will do what He said no matter what, no matter how long it takes. I heard Joel Osteen, Pastor and Author, say *"Faith activates God. Fear activates the Enemy."* Such a true statement. Faith says, *"God will"* and brings Him on the scene. Fear says, *"God may not"* and allows the enemy to bring doubt. Get rid of fear by remembering how many times God came through on your behalf. Say what you believe.

As Long as It Takes

God is faithful to His people. He wants the best for all of us. Therefore, He knows what He's doing in our lives. He just wants us to trust Him. Get rid of doubt and unbelief. Dig in and fight the good fight of faith. (First Timothy 6:12) Declare Psalm 62:1-2, MSG over your life – *"God, the one and only - I'll wait as long as he says. Everything I need comes from him, so why not? He's solid rock under my feet, breathing room for my soul, an impregnable castle: I'm set for life."*

Faithless

God's way of interacting with His people is based on what we don't see in the natural. (Hebrews 11:1) He communicates to us not by what can be seen, but by what is believed in the heart and mind of an individual. Faith is nothing but pure trust and reliability in the One whom you believe. Faith reveals itself in an authentic way when life is challenging and difficult. I'm not challenged to believe God in good times. The challenge is when I can't see my way. Are you full of faith or faithless? *"Faithless is he that says farewell when the road darkens."* (J.R.R. Tolkien, Writer)

Strong Faith

The Bible talks about distinct kinds of faith – great faith, little faith, wavering faith, inconsistent faith. These are levels of our belief system. When we first come to Christ, we have little faith because we are just beginning to know Him. As we grow in grace and in the knowledge of Jesus Christ, our faith becomes more solid. (Second Peter 3:18) But how do you get strong faith? Strong faith is a process. It doesn't come overnight. The more you experience Christ, the more you trust Him. *"Seeds of faith are always within us; sometimes it takes a crisis to nourish and encourage their growth."* (Susan L. Taylor, Writer and Journalist)

FIGHT TO BELIEVE

Every Believer has been given a measure of faith. (Romans 12:3) We didn't have to work for it. Your faith in God will always be challenged. First Timothy 6:12 says *"Fight the good fight of faith, lay hold on eternal life, whereunto thou art also called...."* Belief is power. It is a force that's hard to penetrate. That's why your adversary challenges your belief system. He knows God will do what He says, but he wants you to doubt. The devil is a liar. God is truth. Whose word will you believe? Fight the good fight of faith.

PLEASE GOD BY FAITH

We tend to want the benefit of something without meeting the requirement. I love how God explains Himself in who He is and what He likes and dislikes. Hebrews 11:6 says *"But without faith it is impossible to please him: for he that cometh to God must believe that he is, and that he is a rewarder of them that diligently seek him."* Your 24/7 walk with God is a faith walk. You must deal with God in the realm of faith. If you trust Him, you will believe Him. If you know Him, you will trust Him. Increase your relationship with God by trusting Him even more. Faith is what really pleases Him.

PEACE BRINGS HEALING

God is very intentional. Everything He created, made and formed was purposeful. Not only that, He knew the challenges we would encounter, and made provision for them. We truly have everything we need to live victorious in this world. Who would think God's peace could heal our bodies? Proverbs 14:30, NLT says *"A peaceful heart leads to a healthy body; jealousy is like cancer in the bones.*" This scripture has the power to de-stress you. When you allow God's peace to permeate your heart, it will bring peace to your entire body. His peace will calm your heart and settle you down. If you want a peaceful heart, allow the peace of God to replace all your fears and anxieties.

Perfecting
FINANCES

THE SOURCE

I remember the year I got *really* serious with God about my finances. I did all the things the scriptures told me. I would experience some intermittent financial blessings, but nothing significant enough to break the cycle of lack. I wanted to get to the root of why the scriptures were not working for me. I believed, declared and expected, but something was missing. I knew God couldn't lie. I began to look within myself. That's when the Holy Spirit revealed to me that at the age of 16, I made an *inner vow* that I would never depend on anyone for anything due to constant disappointments. That's how I lived my life. It spilled over into my relationship with God. If He didn't come through, I would make it happen. God allowed me to come to the end of myself. It was only then I realized I couldn't take care of myself. That's when I allowed Him to be my Source. My dependence is on Him in *all* things. I allow Him to give me wisdom and strategies as to how to manage my financial affairs. Oh, the joy that floods my soul!! Let Him be your Source.

MONEY

Does money have you or do you have money? That's an imposing question. It's asked to reveal money's influence and purpose in your life. The Bible says, ***"the love of money is the root of all evil."*** (First Timothy 6:10) Are you at a place in life where you're not attached to money? Or are you so consumed with having it that you will do anything to get it? Money comes and goes. It's a medium of exchange to get what's needed in your life. Stop being so emotionally driven by money and exercise self-control. Learn to be content in whatever state you're in until things change. (Philippians 4:11) Don't let money control you, you control it.

FINANCIAL STRATEGIES

I bet if I were to ask how many people want to get out of debt, everybody's hand would go up. We all want to be debt free, but it's going to take more than you receiving a lump sum of money to address your financial woes. There was a time when everybody wanted God to release millions into our hands so we could be distribution centers. Well, it may have happened for a few, but not for the majority. Before God can entrust you with tremendous financial wealth, you must be disciplined and faithful in what you already have. If you're out of control with your money now, having more will only amplify that. ***"For every financial problem you're fighting God is going to give you a strategy. Get your heart and emotions out of it. Your financial breakthrough and blessing are in the strategy."*** (Amira Scott, Minister and Entrepreneur)

DISCIPLINE

Discipline is difficult while living in a loose world. The economy races like an out-of-control rollercoaster ride when the debt ratio increases. Yet when information is shared concerning budgeting, fiscal management, cutbacks, etc. we reject it because we don't want to be told what to do with our money. I want to challenge you to save some money. See – you immediately rejected that based on what you say you don't have. For one month put all your loose silver change in a container. At the end of the month count it to see how much you saved. You just disciplined yourself to save. *Money comes* but what are you doing with it? Proverbs 13:11 says ***"Dishonest money dwindles away, but he who gathers money little by little makes it grow."***

Perfecting LIFE

PEACE IN THE MIDST

Life can be like a three-ring circus or a classroom full of kids out of control. Life doesn't always present itself with the best of situations. The scriptures tell us that in this life we are going to have trials, tribulations, frustrations, etc. But the scriptures also say that Jesus is the Prince of Peace. He's not just my Lord, Savior, Provider, but He is also in charge of peace. He specializes in peace. If you want peace go to Him. I have a sign on my office wall that says, ***"Peace is not the absence of conflict, but the presence of God."*** The next time your world gets chaotic and crazy, let the Prince of Peace come in. His presence settles everything down! May the God of peace be with you!

A PLAN TO GET YOUR LIFE BACK

Let's take a minute for you to think about you. Where are you going? What are you doing? Do you have a plan for you? I know life might really be demanding right now, but you got to get a grip on it. Don't let life get away from you. Some of you live a sacrificial life for others, but what about you? I'm not talking about not serving or helping. I'm talking about you loosing yourself at the cost of others. You have God-given abilities, gifts and skills that reflect your passion, but you never give attention to them. It's time to acknowledge and nurture them. Work out a step-by-step strategy for what you want to accomplish. Break it down into tiny steps. Focus on the path you need to take. Get your life back!

LIFE'S EXPERIENCES

Mess ups, trip ups, hang ups – tired of it all! Keep stumbling over the same block – when will it ever end? Life falling apart when it should be held together! Do good for a while, then go bad! Content in life – content in Christ then frustration comes to upset everything! Say all the right things, believe sincerely in your heart, do what's required and seems like nothing changes! Let me encourage you. The falling apart, mistakes, failures, etc. are a part of life. *If you don't experience them, you don't learn. If you don't learn, you'll never change!*

LIVING

Life can be so demanding that you can forget its purpose. The main purpose of life is to live. What is living? Living is seizing valuable moments in life. Well, what are valuable moments? The laughter of a child. Feeling a cool evening breeze on a summer night. Closing your eyes and soaking in the tub. Taking your time eating your favorite ice cream. Listening to the birds sing. A good laugh. Being happy for somebody else. Genuinely helping someone in need. Appreciating God's creation. Giving wise counsel. *"Life is a journey – not a destination. Enjoy the trip!"* (Unknown)

ONE DAY AT A TIME

There should be a time at the end of each day that you reflect on all you did. Did your day make a difference in someone's life? Did you learn something new? Did you take time to appreciate the good someone did for you? Could you hear God speak to you through various situations or circumstances? Could you have done anything to make the day better? How was your attitude? Did your conversation add to or take away from? Were you a blessing? Don't worry if the day didn't go like you wanted it. Don't even worry if you missed the mark. *"There is tomorrow – just learn from today!"* (Theresa Scott, Author and Teacher)

THE PAST

A major lesson I have learned in life is - let go of the past. I can't go back and change it, so I've learned to let it go. There's nothing to go back to. Now if I could bring my once youthful body into my present age that would be fantastic. But the mind is connected to the body and I don't want that immature mindset. So, the past stays in the past. If you tend to continually re-visit your past – be it good or bad – consider this: *"Your past is a place of reference, not of residence."* (Willie Jolley, Author) Your residence (where you live) is not the past. You don't live there anymore. You live in your *now* and are on your way to your *future. Let go of the past and the past will let go of you!*

TIMES AND SEASONS

Ecclesiastes 3:1 says *"To everything there is a season, and a time to every purpose under the heaven."* Then after this scripture there are 28 events of life listed. You know – *"a time to be born, a time to die; a time to plant and a time to pluck up that which has been planted"* and so on. Everybody experiences these events at one time or another. When we fully understand this, these events should not throw us out of the arena of life. Your life consists of times and seasons. These are not permanent events. In some form or another your life changes. Stop resisting change – it's the process of life!

DO WHAT YOU CAN

Life can be overwhelming. We see problems all around us. It's easy to throw up our hands in hopelessness. We need not feel responsible for the problems in the world. We are only responsible for our tiny corner of it. If everyone took care of their tiny corner, that would change the world. Analyze your environment – city, town, or block. Think about what needs to be done and do one small thing to get the ball rolling. **"Do what you can, with what you have, where you are."** (Theodore Roosevelt, 26th President of the United States)

ORDER IN LIFE

My neighbor's husband died. He had been sick off and on for six years and had been diagnosed with Alzheimer's. His symptoms progressed to the point he didn't recognize his wife of 46 years. During his illness, she told me she was getting his personal affairs in order and making adjustments in the house. It reminded me of the word the prophet told ailing King Hezekiah *"set your house in order."* (Second Kings. 20:1) My neighbor was not writing her husband off, but knew she needed to get some things in order. Is your house in order? What do you need to do to get on top of personal affairs concerning you or a loved one? We really don't know what life will bring us, but let's get our affairs in order physically and spiritually.

FLOW OF LIFE

It saddens my heart when I see people living an unproductive life. They live aimlessly with no direction or purpose. You were created to do something meaningful. We are all called by God. His hand is on each of us. God is not hiding His will from you concerning your life. It's not a secret. Let's get in the flow of life. Be like Jesus by going about doing *good*. Jesus was a natural and so are you. *"Be helpful. When you see a person without a smile, give them yours."* (Zig

Ziglar, Author and Motivational Speaker) You got the call of God on your life. The least you can do is *smile!*

YESTERDAY

Did you know that *"procrastination is the art of keeping up with yesterday"*? (Don Marquis, Humorist and Author) You will never live in the *now* or move toward the *future* because of constant procrastination. Break the habit of delaying things for another time. Procrastination hinders progress in life. Stop avoiding what's needful. Yesterday is gone. It can never be re-lived. All you have is today and the time ahead of you. Learn from your past, don't live in it. No more procrastination. Manage the affairs of your life *today!*

NEW DAY

With the dawning of each new day comes challenges of all kinds. Life can take you by surprise. The key is how you handle it, so it won't overtake you. Begin your day knowing you are not facing it alone; God is with you. No matter what you encounter. the grace of God will get you through it. Give this day your best which is all that's required. Remember there is tomorrow. John Wayne, American Actor, once said – *"Tomorrow is the most important thing in life. It comes into us at midnight very clean. It's perfect when it arrives, and it puts itself in our hands. It hopes we've learned something from yesterday."* You can make every day a better day by learning from yesterday!

TODAY

It's an awkward place to find yourself - between your past and your future. It's like living in two different worlds. One world is filled with past events and streets lined with what should've and could've been. The other world is filled with great expectations and hope for the future. So here you are sitting in the middle being tortured by the past and the future. All the while your present is getting away from you. Stop everything. Look at where you are right now. *"What lies behind you and what lies in front of you, pales in comparison to what lies inside of you."* (Ralph Waldo Emerson, Essayist and Poet) Let go of the past and everything connected to it. Today allow God's goodness (abilities) in you to arise to lead you into your future (destiny).

YOUR FUTURE

Are you planning for your future? What can you see yourself doing in the future? Your future doesn't have to be years and years away, it can be the next three to six months. What are you doing now that can make your future better than your present? *"Do something today that your future self will thank you for."* (Sean Patrick Flanery, American Actor and Author) What can you do now that somewhere in the future you will be so glad you did? Think about it. Begin to orchestrate your life now so your future will be more rewarding.

WORDS OF LIFE

Words are powerful. If you are a parent, you know how upsetting it can be when you think your children are not listening to you. We forget they do age appropriate stuff, but they do listen and understand. When they become adults, you'll be surprised how many times they quote you. If you've been a true blue, die hard friend to someone and spoke truth to them, the seeds of your words were planted. They took heed to what you said. Without those words of wisdom in times of need, many lives would have fallen apart. *"Someone is sitting in the shade today because someone planted a tree a long time ago."*

(Warren Buffett, Business Investor and Philanthropist) Leave a legacy of good words spoken in the time of need.

SOUL PROSPERITY

Third John 2 says ***"Beloved, I wish above all things that thou mayest prosper and be in health, even as thy soul prospereth."*** To *prosper* means to succeed. God wants us to prosper in our spirit, soul and body. *Soul prosperity* is to be successful in your thinking, reasoning and mental perception. Your soul encompasses your five senses (hear, taste, see, smell and touch). Soul prosperity requires a new mindset. That means you need to pay attention to *how* you think and *why* you think the way you do. Renewal of the mind is a process which is achievable. Change your mind, change your life.

GOD'S PLANS

Jeremiah 29:11 says ***"For I know the plans I have for you, declares the Lord, plans to prosper you and not to harm you, plans to give you hope and a future."*** God told Israel He had great plans for their lives. His plans included a stable future. Do you have a plan for your life? What are you looking forward to? We had no say in the beginning of our lives. We didn't pick our families or where we lived. But we do have input as to how we live now and how we want our future to be. I don't know about you, but I want every day to count. When I get to the end of my days, I want to look back seeing the plan of God carried out.

PLANS AND GOALS

One of the most meaningful things a person can do in life is to make plans and have goals to accomplish something. This shows you have carefully and methodically considered ways to accomplish them. It's a beautiful thing to see a plan come together. Plans and goals are the blueprints for your destination. What really counts is the journey you take to accomplish them. The journey may be long and tedious, but you will appreciate it in the end. Proverbs 16:9 says *"In his heart a man plans his course, but the Lord determines his steps."* You may plan it, but trust God to get you there.

SUCCESS

We all have a desire to be successful in life. Success comes with a price. Success is not for lazy, mediocre people. Success lies in the bosom of adamant, purpose driven individuals. It's challenging work. The work may be hard, but the results are rewarding. *"There are no secrets to success. It is the result of preparation, hard work, and learning from failure."* (Colin Powell, Former National Security Advisor) Save your time and money analyzing successful people. Their lives are a no-brainer – work, work, work. Get busy!

LIVE

God is the giver of life. Not only does He give us life, but He gives us an abundant life in Him. He enables us to live a life in union with His will and purpose for us. He gives us life, but we must live the life. How we live it is on us. *"The best day of your life is the one on which you decide your life is your own. No apologies or excuses. No one to lean on, rely on, or blame. The gift is yours. It is an amazing journey and you alone are responsible for the quality of it. This is the day your life really begins."* (Bob Moawad, Author) Live!

SUCCESS DEFINED

How do you define *success*? Is it having all your needs met? Is it living a life of ease? Is it achieving something great and grandiose?

Is it proving to someone that you're not a failure? The dictionary defines *success* as a favorable outcome; accomplishment of something aimed at; or the attainment of wealth or fame. What is success to you? Let's lay aside what you think you need to be successful and work with what you have right now. *"Put your heart, mind and soul into even your smallest acts. This is the secret to success."* (Swami Sivananda, Hindu Spiritual Teacher) Give your best to all your endeavors. Inward determination will lead to outward success.

SECRET OF SUCCESS

"The secret of success is to know something nobody else knows." (Aristotle Onassis, Business Magnate) The secret of success is to figure out something special and make use of it. This takes a lot of work, study and determination. We think about things every day. Think about your day-to-day life. What is something you dread doing? Think of a way to make it easier or make it fun. You may produce something that can be marketed. In doing so, you become a problem solver. I challenge you to think about your abilities. You are the innovative solution to a perplexing problem.

CIRCUMSTANCES

Life is filled with all sorts of circumstances. Well, what is a *circumstance*? A *circumstance* is an occurrence or condition. It's something that relates to or affects an event. Life is filled with occurrences or conditions that are out of our control. Then there are occurrences or conditions that we caused to happen. *"We are a product of the choices we make, not the circumstances that we face."* (Roger Crawford, Author and Motivational Speaker) If you take careful note of your life, you can see where your choices led to circumstances that could have been prevented. God knows all about it. He already made provision for it when He said, *"my grace is sufficient."* (Second Corinthians 12:9)

LIFE THOUGHTS

Life is what you make of it. The Bible says God has *"given us all things that pertain to life and godliness."* (Second Peter 1:3) You have everything within you to live a full life. How you think about your life will determine how you live it. *"Watch your thoughts; they become words. Watch your words; they become actions. Watch your actions; they become habits. Watch your habits; they become character. Watch your character; it becomes your destiny."* (Frank Outlaw, Actor and Author)

WISDOM DEFINED

The Book of Proverbs in the Bible is full of wisdom on how to live. Believers should make it a point to read a proverb or two weekly to live a better life. The definition of *wisdom* is experience and knowledge together with the power of applying them. We need to take heed to the experiences coupled with knowledge enabling us with the power to live right. God blessed Solomon with supernatural godly wisdom surpassing man's understanding. Empower your life by taking heed to the Book of Proverbs.

GOD'S WISDOM

The Book of Proverbs in the Bible tells us that wisdom cries out to us. (Proverbs 8-9) What makes a person cry? Crying is an emotional expression of joy or sadness. It's an outward demonstration of an inner urge. All of us need the wisdom of God in our daily living. *Wisdom* is defined as experience and knowledge together with the power of applying them. God makes His wisdom known to us by simply asking Him. He has designated an entire Book on wisdom. Allow those godly proverbs to keep you from living foolishly.

NEW THING

God wants to do a *new thing* in you. That *new thing* is to reveal more of Him to you so you can fulfill your purpose. The more you know about Him, the more you know about yourself. Where you are now in Christ is not the sum total of your life in Him. He wants you to experience so much more. So, forget the former things. (Philippians 3:13) Stop confining God to your past experiences with Him. Open your mind, heart and spirit for the new thing He is longing to do in you.

MAKE THE MOST OF LIFE

Waiting for God to manifest His promise involves a process. Paul said in Philippians 4:11 he had to learn to be content in his present state. King Solomon said in Ecclesiastes 5:18-20, MSG *"... here's what I've decided is the best way to live: Take care of yourself, have a good time, and make the most of whatever job you have for as long as God gives you life. And that's about it. That's the human lot. Yes, we should make the most of what God gives, both the bounty and the capacity to enjoy it, accepting what's given and delighting in the work. It's God's gift! God deals out joy in the present, the now. It's useless to brood over how long we might live."*

THE MIND

I know you've heard the saying – *"the mind is a terrible thing to waste."* The Bible says – *"as he thinketh in his heart so is he."* (Proverbs 23:7) Your mind controls the quality of your life. We need the Holy Spirit to lead and guide us. If we don't develop a mind to cooperate with Him, we will never profit from His counsel and guidance. Your mind houses your perception about God, life and people. If you're going to be Christ-minded, you must change the way you think. Francis Quarles, English Poet, said, *"My mind's my kingdom.*" You have the power to rule and reign in your mind. Keep your head clear!

ADDICTED TO AFFLICTIONS

The Bible is full of scriptures that talk about afflictions – *"many are the afflictions of the righteous, but the Lord delivers them out of them all."* (Psalm 34:19) *"In the world you shall have tribulation but be of good cheer; I [Jesus] have overcome the world.* (John 16:33) *"When thou passeth through the waters, I will be with thee; and through the rivers, they shall not overflow thee; when thou walkest through the fire, thou shalt not be burned."* (Isaiah 43:2) Afflictions are inevitable and no one is exempt. Our assurance is that God will bring us out. Some people become addicted to afflictions in order to receive sympathy, gain attention, have an excuse for not fulfilling purpose, and so on. Afflictions are temporary. Get on with life!

SAVED TO BE CHANGED

Have you been changed since you've been saved? Are you really saved, or should I say born again? It's time for self-examination. In the book *"Grace"* written by Bob Lenz, Christian Communicator and Author, he poses the inquiry this way – *"Can you define the focus, intent, purpose and drive of your heart. Is Christ at the center of your world? Do you talk to Him daily? Does He talk to you about what you're supposed to do, who you're supposed to look like and where you're supposed to have your focus? It's got to be Christ. Meeting Jesus changes a person. You can't stay the same."*

PROCESS OF CHANGE

Life is filled with change. Change is necessary to make things better. The more you learn, the more you change. Your cell phone changes every six months. Your Smartphone gets smarter. The iPhone becomes more informed. Change also involves the discovery of creativity. The more you discover, the more you can exercise the creative abilities within you. Since the world and the things in it change regularly for the sake of improvement, what about you? Are you allowing change to improve your life?

I'M THE CHANGE

I don't know about you, but I've been looking for some things to change in my life, family, community, state and country. Things can't keep going like they've been. When will somebody rise and make the changes needed? Does anybody notice the dilemma we're in? Does anybody care? We've amassed technology and gained knowledge about everything. So why aren't things better? Well, I need to change my perspective. Before there can be an outward change there must be an inward change. *"Change will not come if we wait for some other person or some other time. We are the ones we've been waiting for. We are the change that we seek."* (Barak Obama, 44th President of the United States)

YOU GOT ALL YOU NEED

I often hear people say they don't have what they need to live. We base living solely on material possessions. We have measured our lives by the have's and have not's. We compare our lives to the rich and famous. Are we so need-oriented that we have forgotten what life is really all about? God didn't put us on this earth as empty individuals. He created ALL of mankind with creative abilities. He said in Second Peter 1:3 that He *"has given us everything we need for life and godliness."* Your gifts, talents and strengths are all you need to live a full and meaningful life. Look within – your need is met.

PROGRESS IN THE STRUGGLE

In the span of one's lifetime struggles will occur. There are no people on the face of the earth that have not encountered and endured struggles. Each race struggles to be free from something. To *struggle* is to make a determined effort under difficulties. It is to strive hard and to contend with or against something. As we maintain a determined effort under difficulties, we make progress. Don't get caught up in the struggles our forefathers endured, look at the progress they made. Their struggles have afforded us the liberties we now have. Frederick Douglass, Abolitionist and Statesman, said, ***"If there is no struggle there is no progress."*** Keep striving, enduring and achieving for those coming behind you.

DO WHAT'S RIGHT

The world is socialized in negativity. Our Constitution enables us to have free speech. I think the original intent of free speech was to voice what is right and maintain honorable standards. Nowadays we say what we want only to promote human degradation. There will always be issues and problems to bicker over. But when will we make up our minds to turn the tide of negativity and say and do the right thing? If enough of us do and say what is right, wrong is minimized. Let's stop being the product of a negative society and do what's right. In the words of Dr. Martin Luther King, Civil Rights Activist, - ***"The time is always right to do what is right."***

END OF LIFE

Do you ever think about the end of your life? What will people say about you at your funeral? What they say will reflect how you lived. Live your life to the fullest, so at the end of your days people will say you were more than just a good person. I'm not trying to get you to be death conscious, but life conscious. Your life should reflect all that is good in you — all you do to make a difference. You must leave an imprint of your life in the earth. Don't live regretting what you should have done. *"I used to want the words 'She tried' on my tombstone. Now I want 'She did it.'"* (Katherine Dunham, Author and Anthropologist) What will your tombstone say?

SOVEREIGNTY OF GOD

Stress can be defined as anxiety, nervous tension, worry, urgency, etc. Modern medicine has revealed that the results of stress are sleeplessness, chest pains, diarrhea, rapid heartbeat, headaches, and so on. Why do we stress as Christians who know the power of Christ? Is it because we really don't trust God! There is the sovereignty of God and the sovereignty of man. We say, '*God you handle this, and I will handle that.*' That's dual sovereignty. Why do we worry if God is sovereign? If He's not sovereign, then He is not God. There's an old hymn that says, *"Trust and obey for there's no other way."* Trust God with the situation. He knows best.

INSECURITY

If you're struggling with stress it could be due to insecurity. An insecure person is unwilling to say *no, not* or *can't*. This person lives at the convenience of everyone else. They feel more obligated to others than to themselves. They end up losing their self-worth. They are people-pleasers rather than God-pleasers. For those who are insecure in home, work, or, even worse, in God — just *let it go.* Jesus said, *"Come to me all you who labor and are heavy laden and overburdened, and I will cause you to rest. I will ease and relieve and refresh your souls."* (Matthew 11:28, AMP) All God wants you to do is come to Him and *rest!*

STRESS MANAGEMENT 1

There are events and circumstances that bring stress. Some stress is good in that it propels us into what is needed at the time. Then there are other stresses that bring tension, sickness and disease. Therefore, you will not have a stress-free life. Take charge of your life. *"I have set the Lord always before me. Because he is at my right hand, I will not be shaken."* (Psalm 16:8)

STRESS MANAGEMENT 2

How are you handling the stress that comes in your way? Perhaps this can help. Identify what causes stress. When you feel stressed, write down the cause, your thoughts, and your mood. When you discover what's bothering you, develop a plan for addressing it. List all your commitments, assess your priorities, and eliminate any tasks that are nonessential. *"So do not fear, for I am with you; do not be dismayed, for I am your God. I will strengthen you and help you; I will uphold you with my righteous right hand."* (Isaiah 41:10)

STRESS LESS – WALK AWAY

How are you handling the stress that comes your way? Consider this – walk away when you're angry. Before you react, take time to regroup by counting to ten. Then reconsider or reassess the situation. Walking or other physical activities can also help you work off some steam. Exercise increases the production of endorphins which is your body's natural mood-booster. Commit to some type of daily exercise. This makes a dramatic difference in reducing stress levels. *"You are my hiding place; you will protect me from trouble and surround me with songs of deliverance."* (Psalm 32:7-8)

Stress Less – Rest

Have you considered resting your mind? I read a survey that indicates stress keeps more than 40% of adults lying awake at night. You need seven to eight hours of sleep. So cut back on caffeine, remove distractions (e.g. television and computer in your bedroom). Go to bed the same time each night. Engage in exercises that bring relaxation. These are stress reducers that can boost your immune system. *"My soul finds rest in God alone; my salvation; he is my fortress; I will never be shaken."* (Psalm 62:1-2)

Precious Moments

I came across a quote that really caught my attention. It said, *"We do not remember days, we remember moments."* (Cesare Pavese, Italian Poet and Novelist) We get so caught up in the cares of life that we miss precious moments. God created this earth and everything in it for us to enjoy. Jesus said He came so we could have life and it more abundantly. (John 10:10) An abundant life is not solely a materialistic life but a life where there is peace within and without. I embraced a precious moment one day on my lunch hour. I sat in my car with the windows down and closed my eyes while enjoying a cool breeze. I listened to the birds singing. I experienced peace and a refreshing. How many God-given moments have you missed to sense His presence?

Do Your Best

We have been blessed with this one life to live. How we live it is on us. My prayer and desire for you is to have no regrets at the end of your days. May you come to a place in life that you give it your daily best. *"Always do your best. Your best is going to change from moment to moment; it will be different when you are healthy as opposed to sick. Under any circumstance, simply do your best, and you will avoid self-judgment, self-abuse and regret."* (Don Miguel Ruiz, Mexican Author) May we all say to the Lord – *'I gave life my best.'*

VISION

What kind of vision do you have for your life? *Vision* involves what you see in your mind's eye. Your vision should be based on the strengths and passions you have within. You may have a bona fide physical disability but can envision yourself doing remarkable things despite that disability. Don't let your present circumstance limit your desires in life. God gave us an imagination to envision greater and better. Now don't get stuck with vision. Vision must take on manifestation. *Take steps to get vision out of your mind into reality.* **"Vision without execution is just hallucination."** (Henry Ford, Industrialist) It's time for you to execute your vision.

PREPARATION

So often I hear people say, *'this is my season,'* *'this is my turn,'* or *'this is my time.'* We all want our time of opportunities, breakthroughs, and greatness. We all want life to be better right now. But if *better* were to come to you at this very moment, would you be prepared for it? Your *'turn'* – your *'time'* must be preceded with some preparation. If you are expecting to be blessed with a new job, you need to clean up your act on your current job, update your resume, get reliable references, etc. You shouldn't be caught scrambling at the last minute getting these things in order. **"The secret of success in life is for a man to be ready for his opportunity when it comes."** (Benjamin Disraeli, Former Prime Minister of the United Kingdom)

UNPREDICTABLE

Life is unpredictable. It's filled with unexpected events. A series of unpredictable events can get old after a while. At some point you yearn for non-eventful seasons. Instead of allowing those unpredictable times to do you in, you must get a revelation as to how to manage them. This quote says it best – *"If it doesn't challenge you, it doesn't change you."* (Fred DeVito, Entrepreneur) You must now realize God was using these unpredictable times to conform you into His image and likeness. It presented you with challenges you could only face with Him. It brought you closer to Him. It produced a strength in you unrealized at that time. Wow! You're better, so much better!

INTENTIONAL

This year, month, day, hour, minute, second is all you have to do right by God. In doing right by God I mean being intentional in operating in your gifts, going about doing good, and allowing Him to conform you into His image. If you are truly a Christian, then the world around you needs to see it. What are your intentions? What do you intend to do with what God has endowed you with? He saved you to change you and to use you. Intend to live a life that is pleasing to God and not to yourself.

INHERITANCE

For those of you who have children you think about their future – who they will be, what they will achieve, etc. Parents want to be able to leave their children an inheritance of some type to make their lives better once they are gone. Trust funds are good. Being a beneficiary of a sizeable insurance policy is also good. But what about leaving them an inheritance of wisdom, right living, Godly standards and good morals? The money will be long gone, but sound life principles will last a lifetime. *"My hope for my children must be that they respond to the still, small voice of God in their own hearts.* "(Andrew Young, Former United States Representative and Civil Rights Activist)

LIFE IS A LESSON LEARNED

Life is filled with experiences. Some experiences make sense while others leave us saying *hmm.* Life has a way of teaching us valuable lessons. Life experiences reveal strengths and weaknesses. They mature us. They break us down and build us back up. They reveal the raw truth concerning matters of our heart. We know wisdom comes from God, but also from life experiences. I always say *life is a lesson learned.* We had to experience the situation to learn valuable lessons that changed the trajectory in our lives. What has life taught you? Did it make you better or bitter? Learn from your experiences so you can live a fulfilled life.

WISE COUNSEL

People don't like to be told what to do, but they seek advice. Sounds crazy but that's how we are. We don't like to be told that what we're doing is wrong. We don't like counsel that brings correction. We don't like counsel that challenges us. Well, like it or not, here's some wise counsel from Proverbs 4:20-23 – *"My son pay attention to what I say; listen closely to my words. Do not let them out of your sight, keep them within your heart; for they are life to those who find them and health to a man's whole body. Above all else, guard your heart, for it is the wellspring of life."* Wise counsel saves your life!

BENEFIT OF WISE COUNSEL

If you live long enough you will realize you don't know everything. You need the advice/counsel of someone else. When I seek counsel, I want to get it from someone who has some knowledge of what I need – some experience if you will. First, I go to God who knows everything about me and ask for His wisdom. Second, He either tells me or directs me to where I need to go. Some counsel is easy to be entreated. Other counsel may take a moment to process. Never get to a place in life where you think you don't need counsel. Proverbs 3:7-8 says ***"Do not be wise in your own eyes; fear the Lord and shun evil. This will bring health to your body and nourishment to your bones."*** Wise counsel produces a healthy lifestyle.

ATTITUDE

Life consists of the good, bad and ugly which are strong influences. Good makes you feel good – it's a positive influence. Bad makes you feel bad – it's a negative influence. Ugly makes you feel ugly – out of sorts and contrary. These influences affect your attitude. Your attitude displays your state of mind. You don't have to say a thing – your attitude reveals it. A good attitude reveals positive actions. A bad attitude reveals negative actions. How do you handle a bad attitude? ***"A bad attitude is like a flat tire – you can't go anywhere until you change it."*** (Unknown)

CONQUERING

"Success is to be measured not so much by the position that one has reached in life as by the obstacles which he has overcome while trying to succeed." (Booker T. Washington, Orator and Author) Life is full of challenges, situations, setbacks and so on. You can't avoid it, so you might as well learn how to handle them. Overcoming each challenge makes you stronger and more confident. Challenging times in life reveal what's really in you. God is with you and will always remind you that you are *"more than a conqueror."* (Romans 8:37)

INSIDE YOU

You've heard the saying – *"you can't keep a good man (woman) down."* That refers to someone who made it through a rough time in life. They experienced a hardship and survived. It almost took them out, but they came back strong. That should be said about all of us. There's an inner strength and a determination in all of us to beat the odds against us. Some may call it willpower. But if you're in Christ you have the grace of God to get you through any and everything because greater is He that is *in* you than he that is in the world. (First John 4:4) You are *more than a conqueror*. Don't accept defeat another day. *"I survived because the fire inside me burned brighter than the fire around me."* (Joshua Graham, Mormon Missionary and Author)

Perfecting
PRAYER

PRAYER

James 5:13 says *"Is any among you afflicted? Let him pray."* Another translation says *"Is any one of you in trouble? He should pray."* Yet another translation says *"Is anyone among you afflicted (ill-treated, suffering evil)? He should pray."* We are our brother's keeper in that we are held responsible to pray for them when they are afflicted, in trouble, ill-treated or suffering evil. *PRAY* – not gossip or talk about them. They are not in sin. Evil is trying to overtake them. Don't ignore it or complain about it another day – *PRAY. PRAY* them through as you would want to be prayed through. Go to your Heavenly Father on their behalf and get the devil off their back!

STRONG PRAYER

We go through seasons of consistency and inconsistency in prayer. It all depends on what's happening at the time. Adversities and challenges will bring you to your knees. Good, happy and peaceful times tend to lessen our intensity in prayer. The Bible tells us to pray without ceasing. (First Thessalonians 5:17) No matter what the season is in your life, prayer must be continually lifted up to your Father. These can be prayers of thanksgiving, petitions, intercession, etc. Think about this when you drift off into complacency – *"Pray as though everything depended on God. Work as though everything depended on you."* (Saint Augustine, Theologian and Philosopher)

BECOMING ONE WITH PRAYER

There are numerous benefits of prayer. This is our link with God. Prayer is empowerment. This comes from us connecting with God – uniting and yielding to the Holy Spirit. Mark 11:23-24 says *"What things soever ye desire when ye pray believe that you receive them and ye shall have them."* *Believing* is connecting yourself with prayer. It is becoming *one* with prayer. When you *connect* in prayer you lock yourself in with what you believe and leave no room for doubt, fear or unbelief. Let your prayers come from a place where you pray *"Lord make me one with Your will in this prayer request."* This will release His will, not yours!

HEART MATTER

I have learned over the years that God is always concerned about our motives and what's really in our heart. That's one of the reasons we say serving God is relational and not religious. It's not about a bunch of do's and don'ts. We are to serve God with our whole heart. That means we give Him our all. Too often we get caught up in the demands of life and find ourselves praying more for our needs rather than honoring and worshipping the One who meets the need. Do an inventory of your prayer life. Check to see if you're asking more than worshipping. Are you serving God merely for what He can do for you or serving Him for who He is?

Perfecting
PURPOSE & GIFTS

GOD'S ORIGINAL INTENT

Purpose is a thing intended. What did God have on His mind when He called His people? A people belonging to the Lord. (Deuteronomy 7:6-7) A treasured possession. A kingdom of priests. A holy nation. (Exodus 19:5-6) Chosen generation, royal priesthood, peculiar people (First Peter 2:9) These are characteristics of an elite group of people governed by a higher standard of living. Therefore, in the Kingdom of God you must learn what is required of you. You also must qualify to effectively walk in these positions. That's called process. Process is a series of changes. These are changes for character development. *"The steps of a good man are ordered by the Lord and he delighteth in his way."* (Psalm 37:23)

PURPOSE DEFINED

God created you with a purpose. He said *"For I know the plans I have for you, declares the Lord, plans to prosper you and not to harm you, plans to give you hope and a future. Then you will call upon me and come and pray to me, and I will listen to you. You will seek me and find me when you seek me with all your heart. I will be found by you declares the Lord."* (Jeremiah 29:11-14, NIV) We have a way of asking others about our purpose. They can only give their opinion. Since they did not create you, their opinion may be a little off. Only God knows why He created you. I encourage you to go to your Creator so He can show you great and mighty things about your life.

DOMINION

God's original intent for man was to be fruitful, multiply, replenish, subdue and have dominion in the earth. (Genesis 1:28) He said in Psalm 115:16 that *"the heavens are the Lord's: but the earth hath he given to the children of men."* He rules the heavens. We have dominion in the earth. God has power over everything because He is *all* powerful. He gave man authority in the earth. Satan took that authority from man (Adam) in the garden. Jesus Christ came and gave that authority back to us. When was the last time you took authority over diabolical activity in your life?

PECULIAR PEOPLE

I wonder how much of God's Word we really believe and understand. We quote scriptures but are not allowing the scriptures to become a part of us. Case in point. The Bible says we are a *"chosen generation, a royal priesthood, a holy nation, a peculiar people."* (First Peter 2:9) What makes us holy and peculiar? It's not being a holy roller or a weird religious freak. What was God's intention when He chose us? We were to be a nation of people distinguished from all other nations. Deuteronomy 4:5-9 says we are to be a *"great nation"* consisting of *"a wise and understanding people."* And a nation that has *"a God near them whenever they pray to him."* Therefore, stop being ashamed of being a child of God. Stop trying to fit back into the world He brought you out of. You are to be envied above all the peoples of the earth!

You Are God's Product

Ephesians 2:10 says *"For we are God's workmanship, created in Christ Jesus to do good works, which God prepared in advance for us to do."* The New Living Translation says we are God's *"masterpiece."* The word *workmanship* means a thing that is made. It is a product. You are a product God has made. You are His masterpiece which has been artfully crafted. A product has a specific purpose. You are a masterfully, well-crafted product of God that produces good works. Stop living by other people's estimation. Change your mind about who you are. You are God's masterpiece. You are not a piece of junk or someone's mistake. You are of God.

Spiritual Gifts – Be Not Ignorant

God has seen fit to bless all of mankind with at least one gift or ability. These gifts enable us to do various things. He gives to people to benefit each other. A gift is to be given, not kept. Paul takes the time to explain spiritual gifts in First Corinthians 12:1 – *"Now about spiritual gifts brothers, I do not want you to be ignorant."* This is something every believer is to understand. He explains the purpose and intent of the gifts – that the gifts are to benefit others. First Peter 4:10, NLT says *"God has given each of you a gift from his great variety of spiritual gifts. Use them well to serve one another."* Let's not deprive anyone else of the spiritual gifts God has given each of us.

Gift Not Withdrawn

All through the Bible we see men and women who had character flaws, but God still used them. In the Old Testament the Spirit of God came *upon* individuals to carry out His will. In the New Testament the Spirit of God is *within* them to do His will. You may be flawed, but you are still gifted. Romans 11:29 says *"the gifts and callings of God are without repentance."* The New Living

Translation says, ***"For God's gifts and his call can never be withdrawn."*** I come against the spirit of condemnation in your life that holds you in bondage to your slip ups. I bind it and loose it from you. I release the forgiveness of God and say you are still accepted in the beloved. Go and sin no more. You still have something to give!

FLAWED BUT GIFTED

I'm reminded of how many times David operated out of a flawed character. He messed up but kept going back to God. He asked God to put a right spirit in him. God never withdrew His spirit from David as he remained a warrior and king. Peter denied Christ three times. No doubt he experienced tremendous rejection, failure and condemnation. Christ restored him. He did not strip Peter of his calling. Romans 11:29, AMP says – ***"For God's gifts and His call are irrevocable. He never withdraws them once they are given, and He does not change His mind about those to whom He gives His grace or to whom He sends His call."*** Get right with God. Let Him use you again. He gifted and called you – not man!

GIFTED ANYWAY

How well do you know yourself? We describe ourselves by our likes and dislikes. We tend to define ourselves by what others say and how they perceive us. You may say positive things about yourself, but do you really believe what you say? If you did, you would not be struggling with the opinions of others or your own personal negativity. We are gifted but flawed, saved but not totally delivered, and continuously being transformed by the renewing of our minds. It's time for you to genuinely acknowledge yourself along with the greatness God placed in you. ***"We know what we are but know not what we may be."*** (William Shakespeare, Poet, Playwriter and Actor)

CAN'T HIDE

There is a false doctrine, another gospel and misinterpretation of the Word of God that says you can maintain an ungodly lifestyle while anointed. Let's clear the air about being anointed. God has anointed each one of us with a gift. Romans 11:29, AMP says *"For God's gifts and His call are irrevocable. He never withdraws them when once they are given, and He does not change His mind about those to whom He gives His grace or to whom He sends His call."* God is not going to take His gift on your life back. *However*, ungodly character and ungodly behavior can minimize the gift/anointing. God's anointed people are required to display the fruit of the Spirit, forgive, repent, be merciful, etc. You can't hide behind the anointing. The anointing does not exempt you from being holy and treating people right.

MINISTRY GIFTS

The Bible says Jesus gave gifts to the Body of Christ – apostles, prophets, evangelists, pastors and teachers *"for the perfecting of the saints, for the work of the ministry, for the edifying of the body of Christ."* (Ephesians 4:11-12) These are not self-appointed gifts or positions. Jesus gives them. Therefore, if we are not endowed from on high with these gifts, we won't adequately operate in them. I wonder if this is the reason why so many in the Body of Christ aren't perfected/maturing, not taught how to do the work of the ministry, nor edified (built up). Let's get back to God's original intent and focus on operating fully in it.

PERFECTING THE SAINTS

To all who possess God's appointed five-fold ministry gifts (apostles, prophets, evangelists, pastors and teachers) I want to encourage you to be true to your calling. Ephesians 4:12 says the first administration of your gift is to *perfect* the saints. *Perfect* (Greek) means to mend, restore, adjust, repair, complete thoroughly. You have been graced to bring wholeness to people – spirit, soul and body – so they can live a Christ-like life. You're not expected to know how to do it all, but God will show you where to get help. Learn to utilize other gifts in the Body of Christ. The sincere ones don't want your sheep, they just want to help.

PERSON OF VALUE

Albert Einstein, Theoretical Physicist, once said, ***"Try not to become a man of success, but rather try to become a man of value."*** Success achieved in a scrupulous manner can tarnish a person's character. To be a true success, you must be a person with standards and values. What lies beneath your success? When your successful life is examined by others, what will they discover? Let it not be arrogance, pride, haughtiness, greed or selfishness. May you never forget Who caused you to be successful. And because your success did not begin with you, you owe it to God and man to be a person of Godly standards. He is the one who put value in your life.

THE ANOINTING

Isaiah 27:10 says ***"And it shall come to pass in that day, that his burden shall be taken away from off they shoulder and his yoke from off thy neck, and the yoke shall be destroyed because of the anointing."*** God has anointed everybody to do something. The anointing is not only to *do*, but to *be*. For you to be the person God called you to be, He has anointed you not just for others, but also for yourself. There are areas in your life that need to be destroyed. There are things you are yoked up to that need to be displaced. You have the enablement of God to help others. You also have it to help you. The anointing coupled with the Spirit of God can help you overcome all your personal inadequacies.

MAINTAIN YOUR SPIRITUAL GIFTS

It is a wonderful thing to discover the gifts of God in your life. Experiencing His love flowing through you to others is priceless. Possessing gifts and the anointing does not make you a good person. You are still required to be conformed into the image of Christ Jesus. You are gifted but flawed. Don't allow character flaws to contaminate the gifts of God in you. Protect your gift by living right before God and man.

PROTECT THE ANOINTING

God has endowed each of us with the ability to do a specific thing. Everyone is born with a special calling to do good for others. The anointing to carry out the will of God must be protected. Once you discover your gift/calling, it's on you to protect it. It is vital for you to watch who you connect with. You have God's grace to get out of toxic relationships that contaminate you. You don't need anybody in your life to help you do bad. You are God's workmanship. (Ephesians 2:10) He sanctified (set you apart) to carry out His plan. Protect what He has given you. Use it to His glory.

ARISE

Isaiah 60:1-3 says *"Arise, shine for thy light is come, and the glory of the Lord is risen upon thee. For behold the darkness shall cover the earth, and gross darkness the people: but the Lord shall arise upon thee, and His glory shall be seen upon thee. And the Gentiles shall come to thy light, and kings to the brightness of thy rising."* If you are truly born again, and living a life that reflects Him, then you must realize you are His glory in the earth. Glory is light. Light dispels darkness. Light also illuminates. You are being noticed because of the glory of God – shine on!

DOERS

Talk shows, opinions, and freedom of speech is how we exercise our right in America to verbalize how we feel about anything and anybody. If we are unable to exercise this right, we would cease to be the land of the free and home of the brave. The Statue of Liberty was erected to tell the world we are a free democracy. Voicing our opinion is good, but it needs to be backed up with some action. With all our opinions we fail to execute ways to make this nation better. In the words of Leroy Eldridge Cleaver, Writer and Political Activist, ***"You're either part of the solution or part of the problem."*** Let's not be talkers but doers – making a difference.

PROBLEM SOLVER

The late revolutionist Leroy Eldridge Cleaver, Writer and Political Activist, said, ***"You're either part of the solution or part of the problem."*** So, my question to you is which one are you – the problem or the solution? The world is full of people who do nothing but criticize and blame others for all the problems we have. We spend billions of dollars analyzing, assessing and critiquing, but when will someone create a workable solution? People know they're not in right standing with God. They know they're sinners, but who's going to show them a better way? Once the problem has been identified, let's all work on solutions for the betterment of everyone. You are the answer – the problem solver. It's Christ in you the hope of glory.

GOOD LEFTOVERS

"The measure of who we are is what we do with what we have." (Vince Lombardi, Football Player and Coach) You have been endowed with unique abilities and gifts. The thing that caps this ability is comparison. You feel you must measure up to someone else's standards. Your life was never meant to be like someone else. Look within yourself. Take note of your strengths. Glean from your life's experiences which have left you with some profound wisdom. Stop seeing your life as messed up, useless or defeated. You've learned some things along the way. You may have lost some things, but not everything. Work with what remains!

GOD'S DAY

Here I am with a brand new day. I don't know what it will bring me, but here I am. So instead of the day being about everything I have to do, I want this to be a day where I make God happy. *God what can I do to bring You glory? Don't let me pass up opportunities to do good and reflect You in the earth. Help me to let my light shine so men may see my good works and glorify You.* Today is God's day, not mine. How will your day be?

MARKETPLACE WITNESS

This *Perfecting Moment* is for ALL the people who must interact with the public – sales clerks, bank tellers, cashiers, maintenance workers, healthcare workers, bus and taxi drivers, waiters, etc. Some of the jobs we work on are solely for the need of money. Other jobs are a result of the professional training we undertook. No matter what the reason, treat people with respect. A bad and nasty attitude will draw a bad and nasty attitude. When the public hears you complaining about your job that gives them a bad image of you and the company. If you don't like where you work, then quit. Stop making life hard for everybody else. Get yourself together. Straighten up your face! You never know who God will put in front of you to take you to your *'next.'*

PROFITABLE DAY

I'm not sure how you end your day or what you do before going to bed. It should be a time to reflect on the day's activities. Before you crash make a mental assessment of what you did inwardly and outwardly. In all your doing, was it profitable? Did it count or make a positive difference? Consider this – ***"Did I offer peace today? Did I bring a smile to someone's face? Did I say words of healing? Did I let go of my anger and resentment? Did I forgive? Did I love? These are the real questions. I must trust that the little bit of love that I sow now will bear many fruits, here in this world and the life to come."*** (Henri Nouwen, Writer and Theologian)

THE BODY

For quite a few years I've been searching for my ideal house. I have seen houses with tremendous potential but had to count the cost of renovation. I've seen brand new houses with all the bells and whistles, but had to consider a higher mortgage. I want a home with enough space for everything I need to do. One day I know I'll have it. After spending so much time looking for a spacious home, I realized I neglected to take notice of where I'm living now. Not my *physical* house, but my *natural* house – my *body*. That's the house I need to work on to house the things needed for me to finish my assignment. We live in these bodies that can't be replaced. You can't move out of it and get another one. My point – ***"Take care of your body. It's the only place you have to live."*** (Jim Rohn, Entrepreneur and Author)

GREATER WORKS

Why aren't we seeing greater miracles, healings, and deliverances in our local fellowships and in the marketplace? The god of this world has so cleverly drawn us away from the call of God that we've forgotten our assignment. Jesus sent the Holy Spirit to help us do greater works in the earth. Each believer can render miracles, healings and deliverance to those they encounter. That's how we spread the Kingdom of God in the earth. Break your routine. Put down your technical devices. Open your heart and mind to the Lord. Allow Him to flow through you.

TRIUMPH IN HIM

"Thanks be unto God who always causes us to triumph in Christ Jesus." (Second Corinthians 2:14) While meditating on this scripture I can plainly see how God gave me the victory in overcoming obstacles, challenges, and adversities. I didn't understand it all, didn't know how to handle it, didn't have a strategy or plan for surprise attacks, but had enough Holy Ghost sense to know God was with me. As long as I know Him, and He knows me nothing is impossible in life to handle. To God be the glory for empowering us to triumph in the affairs of life!

POWER TO OVERCOME

There are two words Christians need to be incredibly careful in saying – *can't* and *won't*. Unfortunately, we prefer the word *can't*. Any Christian who takes the Bible seriously will have to agree that the word *can't* really should be *won't*. We forget we have been given the power and ability to overcome. We're really saying *I won't* because we don't choose to say, *"With the help of God, I will!"* (*Wisdom for the Way*, Chuck Swindoll, Pastor and Author) Will you say I will this time?

MORE THAN A CONQUEROR

You ever wonder why you have so many battles to fight? Why there are so many obstacles in your way? The Bible says that God *"always causes us to triumph in Christ"* (Second Corinthians 2:14); it's *"God which gives us the victory through our Lord Jesus Christ"* (First Corinthians 15:57); and *"in all these [battles] things we are more than conquerors."* (Romans 8:37) When God made you in His image and likeness, He put an overcoming spirit in you. Every time you are confronted with opposition, something should rise within you to forge ahead. Goliath showed up in David's life to force the king in him to come forth. Your battles are designed to wake up the *king* in you.

YOUR LIFE, YOUR BUSINESS

I bet you didn't know you have your own business. That's right! You are the sole proprietor of your business. Your business is in high demand. People have been looking for it. They have Googled it, inquired on Facebook and at the local Chamber of Commerce, rode around town in search of it, but can't seem to locate it. I wonder if your business lacks exposure. Well, enough of this. Let me tell you what your business is. Your *life* is your business. Your product is the gifts and abilities you have been given in exchange for the betterment of others. Your life is in high demand!

MAKE THE WORLD BETTER

It is your responsibility to choose wisely when it comes to what you will do with *you*. Your life was never meant to be defined by your past or present circumstances. Life presents many obstacles and challenges to us, but it's how we oversee them that make life worth living. The gifts and abilities within you are limitless. Focus more on your God-given abilities. Acknowledge them, own up to them and work them powerfully.

Release Yourself

There's something inside of you that causes unrest, frustration and aggravation. It's not a hormonal change. It's not people, the job or the church. It's not the lack of things or the abundance of things. It's hard to describe, but there's something inside of you that is longing to be released. It's the real you dancing with your passion, calling and abilities. It wants out. It will continue to aggravate you until you release it. What are you waiting for?

Give Yourself Away

Everyone searches for something to bring them satisfaction and fulfillment. I've done it for years, but each time my search ended when I genuinely gave of myself to help others. Me having a positive effect on someone's life was priceless. It brought an indescribable inner joy. No wonder Jesus said, *"My meat is to do the will of him that sent me and to finish His work."* (John 4:34) Giving of yourself along with doing the will of God satisfies more than food or money.

Gifts Make Room

Proverbs 18:16 says *"A man's gift maketh room for him, and bringeth him before great men."* The New International Version of the Bible records it like this *"A gift opens the way for the giver and ushers him into the presence of the great."* The Message Bible reads, *"A gift gets attention; it buys the attention of eminent people."* What is your gift doing for you? Better still, does anyone even know you are gifted? Well, whether you're operating in your gift or not, your gift has the potential to take you where you've never been before. Are you up for the challenge?

Develop Your Gift

For those of you who are operating in your gifts, I want to challenge you to take it to another level. Don't get complacent where you are. It may be good, but there's more. If you want better results in what you're doing, change is inevitable. Seek ways of greater effectiveness and efficiency. Prepare for expansion through further education, increased technology and sound economics. Whether you have a business or service, there is room for improvement. The world is ever changing and improving, what about you?

Perspective

"When you look at a field of dandelions, you can either see a hundred weeds or a hundred wishes." (Unknown) It's all about perspective. When you look at yourself, what do you see? Do you only see your mistakes, failures, or the *coulda-woulda-shoulda*? It's time to change your outlook, conception and perception. Failure is learning what does not work. A mistake is an incorrect idea, opinion or thought which can be corrected. All that other stuff means you still have time to pursue. Change your perspective.

Just Do It

Maya Angelou, American Poet and Author, wrote, *"Talent is like electricity. We don't understand electricity. We use it."* The gifts and abilities in you need not remain stagnant due to you trying to explain them and seek others' approval. Your life must be utilized for it to be of any value. You may *look* good, but are you *doing* anything good? I'm not impressed with what you know, but with what you do. Let's do this thing called *living* to benefit yourself and others.

TAKE TIME

Time is a straightforward way of measuring out our lives. You have the moment you are living in right now. Time can't be managed in terms of controlling it, but you can utilize it better. Ecclesiastes 3:1 says ***"There is a time and a season for every activity under the sun."*** Don't live a life of regret. In this season of it, live your life to the fullest. Seize the moment. *If you don't take time, time will take you.*

Perfecting
RELATIONSHIPS

A FRIEND

Friends are gifts from God. Take a good look at yourself and see you for who you are. You know it takes somebody special to get along with you. You may have a superior estimation of yourself, but you know you're a piece of work. A friend accepts you for who you are. A friend can look pass the bad and see the good. They may not always agree with you, but you can count on them. A friend knows who you are and who they are, but neither are in competition. My friend gave me a desk sign that says, ***"Good friends follow you anywhere."*** (Winnie the Pooh, Disney Fictional Character) I don't talk to her a lot, but I know she's there for me. Thank God for His precious gift – a friend.

BE YOU

I think it's cool to meet new people. Some may not agree with that. When I meet new people, I take note of their uniqueness. When I interact with people I'm familiar with, their uniqueness keeps the relationship going. We all have bags in life filled with crazies, awkward perceptions and habits. Meeting new people is like taking a journey, yet not always knowing where it will lead. At best it will teach you some things you never knew. People are an amazing species. Don't be afraid to interact with new people because they are looking for your uniqueness as well.

ACCEPTANCE

Have you ever felt inferior in someone's presence? That inferiority could not only come from the other person, but from you. The Bible says comparing ourselves with others is not good. (Galatians 6:4) God intentionally made us different. Take time to analyze your own weaknesses and strengths. Accept your uniqueness. You were meant to be different. Be content with you. Anyway, why would you want to be like someone else when you are so fearfully and wonderfully made?

LIVE IN PEACE

In a relationship, it is the desire of everyone to be accepted and respected. Romans 12:18 says **"If it is possible, as far as it depends on you, live at peace with everyone."** *Live at peace* in this scripture means to put an end to strife. What do you do when it's almost impossible to live at peace with someone? It takes two to argue. Since I'm secure in who I am, I have a choice to participate with you or let you show out by yourself. In relationships, I can choose my battles. Why should I lower my standards or jeopardize my posture of peace for your sake? I won't lose face or even feel you can get over on me when I choose to walk away. *I leave you to yourself!*

A FOOL

When you argue with a fool you become a fool. You put yourself on an even plain with him. Don't allow anyone to take you where you don't want to go. The Bible says a **"soft answer turns away wrath."** (Proverbs 15:1) Do the opposite of what is being presented to you. This confounds the other person. You take control of the situation by not lowering your standards. Self-control is a fruit of the Spirit. Here's some wise counsel – *"Raise your words, not your voice. It is rain that grows flowers, not thunder."* (Jalal ad-Din Rumi, Persian Poet)

DIFFICULT PEOPLE TEACHER

God has so orchestrated life that He provided us with special teachers at every juncture. We've all had the **Difficult People Teacher**. I don't know about you, but I hated her class. I flunked that class only to keep taking it until I passed. **Difficult People Teacher** was a hard taskmaster. That class stressed me out. One day while dealing with a difficult person, I remembered what I learned in that class. I can now say *'I'm thankful for all those difficult people in my life, they have shown me exactly who I do not want to be.'* What did you learn from the **Difficult People Teacher**? I hope you learned something; if not, you're gonna take that class again!

BAD RELATIONSHIPS

Relationships start out well with good intentions. Somewhere, somehow and for some reason a relationship can go bad. You may be the victim of an unhealthy relationship. You did all the right things, but it didn't work. No matter what you did you couldn't please the other party. You walked in patience, longsuffering, forgiveness and most importantly the love of God. You looked past faults. You chose to see the good. Despite that they were determined to treat you in a negative way. Well my friend, it's time to draw the line. Draw a boundary line. Guard your heart. You can only be responsible for you, not for the actions of others. *Even a dog gets tired of being beaten!*

CRITICISM

I'm sure in your years of living you have had some clever ideas, and inspirations. You were motivated to do something really good. You shared it with someone who found fault with it. That shut you down. Why did you allow that? That was your idea, your passion, your inspiration, your motivation. Critics or fault finders are all around us. We can't avoid them. ***"To avoid criticism, do nothing, say nothing, and be nothing."*** (Elbert Hubbard, Writer and Publisher) Your ideas and inspirations are meant to help somebody. Don't let them down!

CONSTRUCTIVE CRITICISM

I've learned a lot from my critics also known as fault finders. I've also learned that no matter what good the Lord has me to do, someone will find fault with it. If I stopped at every juncture of a criticism, I would be most miserable. So instead of shutting down, I turned *negative criticism* into *constructive criticism*. Negativity taught me how to stand up to it and keep believing in what I needed to do. I turned *no* into *yes*; *no way* into *some way*; *can't* into *can*; *will not* into *will*. You get my drift. ***"A successful man is one who can lay a firm foundation with the bricks that others throw at him."*** (Sidney Greenberg, American Rabbi and Author)

RESPECT

George Washington Carver, Scientist and Inventor, once said ***"How far you go in life depends on your being tender with the young, compassionate with the aged, sympathetic with the striving and tolerant of the weak and strong. Because someday in your life you will have been all of these."*** The point here is - be considerate of one another. Regardless of age or generational gaps, we must all strive to treat each other with respect. We live in a disrespectful society that is reaping what it has sown. Disrespect has caused grave misunderstandings and the shedding of innocent blood. Disrespect begets disrespect and respect begets respect. If you want to be respected, respect others. You never know who you may need in life.

FOOL

What is the definition of a *fool?* A *fool* is a person who acts or thinks unwisely or imprudently. It's a stupid person — a clown, a cheat, a deceiver. Proverbs 12:15 says ***"The way of a fool seems right to him, but a wise man listens to advice."*** The Message Bible translates that wisdom like this, ***"Fools are headstrong and do what they like; wise people take advice."*** I know you're not a fool but look at your actions and reactions. Are you headstrong — doing what you want at the expense of others? Are you irrational in handling your affairs? Stop living like a fool. Think before you act. Get some sound advice. *You don't know everything!*

GIVE LIFE

I was checking on a friend of mine one day to see how she was doing. She told me had been helping a friend whose daughter passed the previous year. She had been helping to rearrange furniture and fix the house up. This was a particularly challenging time for both because the one who was helping the other had experienced the loss of a loved one as well. I noted how helping others gets us through challenging times. If you know someone who is mentally, emotionally or spiritually struggling, extend a helping hand. It's not about giving money, but taking time with someone who could really use a lift.

PURPOSE OF RELATIONSHIPS

I engaged in a business relationship that I failed to end in a timely manner. It was on the verge of getting quite ugly. I had to come to the realization that relationships are for times and seasons. This is what God told me, it might help you – *"What stunts your growth is your reluctance and unwillingness to sever relationships or end them in a timely manner. You continue in it, thinking it will get better. You ignore all the warning signs saying, 'termination inevitable.' You stay in it too long. Then I have to come and cut it because it slows up the progress of My plans for your life. It's not the individual but the purpose of the relationship that must be discerned and understood."* Selah!

CHANGE IN RELATIONSHIPS

Relationships can become complex when we overlook each other's growth and maturity. Most of the people in your circle have been there for a substantial period. Neither one of you are the same as you were in the beginning. Life's challenges hopefully mature you. We grow at different paces and in different directions. Relationships mature over the process of time. Therefore, we need to treat each other with greater respect in these new levels of growth and maturity. Stop expecting relationships to remain the same. **"People change and forget to tell each other."** (Lillian Hellman, American Playwright) Communicate your change in your relationships. It's time for everybody to grow up!

UNCONDITIONAL LOVE

We all want to be loved. If we say otherwise, we're lying! You can love God and yourself, which is good, but there's a part of you that needs to be loved. That's not a sign of weakness. God made us relational. The love of others connects us. This relational love can prove to be challenging. God gives us His unconditional love for each other. In the words of Hugh Mackay, Australian Psychologist and Author, – **"Nothing is perfect. Life is messy. Relationships are complex. Outcomes are uncertain. People are irrational."** I want to encourage you to keep loving, caring, and forgiving. If God can unconditionally love you, you can do the same to others.

RELATIONAL GOD

We serve a God who is relational. His original intent was to always have fellowship with man. Out of that fellowship we were to have meaningful relationships with each other. God gave Moses instructions for the children of Israel about how they were to treat each other. (Deuteronomy 15, 19) Jesus came and taught in the Beatitudes (Matthew 5) how kingdom relationships should be. The world is to recognize us by the love we have for each other. (John 13:35) Relationships matter to God.

GENUINE INTERACTION

Communication and effective relational interaction are vital in the work of the ministry. The day is over where we complain about who we can and cannot have a good relationship with. Enhancing our relationships requires mastery and skill. *"It is not our purpose to become each other; it is to recognize each other, to learn to see the other and honor him for what he is."* (Hermann Hesse, German Poet and Novelist)

TRUST IN RELATIONSHIPS

"Nothing is perfect. Life is messy. Relationships are complex. Outcomes are uncertain. People are irrational." (Hugh Mackay, Australian Psychologist and Author) If we aren't careful, the lack of knowledge in relationships can cause distrust and withdrawal. But that's not how life is to be. We take risks in interactions with each other, hoping to be accepted for who we are. Don't withdraw yourself

from people because of trust issues or an unpleasant experience. God is perfecting those things that pertain to you. (Psalm 138:8)

REJECTION

We all have a desire to be accepted for who we are and what we have to say. Our lives are meaningful. We have something to offer. That being the case, why do we allow rejection to sit us down and snatch the very purpose of our existence? Well, I want to encourage you with this – ***"Don't feel bad if someone rejects you. People usually reject expensive things because they can't afford them."*** (Unknown) Maintain your personal worth and value. Don't sell yourself cheap. You are not a bargain. You are an original brand and can't be discounted.

NO MORE VICTIM

It's so easy to blame others for the plights in our lives. Some of you are victims of a tough situation. In the eyes of the world you have every right to be angry, upset and revengeful. After all, it wasn't your fault. Well, it may not have been your fault, but it's time for you to stop giving that bad situation power. Stop rehearsing it. Stop talking about it. Don't let a past power keep you in bondage. You've got your whole life *before* you. Come to grips with the fact you've been shacking up with *victimization* far too long. It's time to end the relationship. Pack up their stuff and put them out. Let God heal you everywhere you hurt. Determine to say what He says about you and *live*!

SINGLES

For several years, I've been on an assignment to intercede for some singles God placed in my life. There have been no manifestations of the opposite sex yet. But let me tell you they have had some camouflages. Who they thought might have been THE ONE - was not! Some of the singles experienced major disappointments. They experienced some heartbreaking moments as well. Others tried to make it happen, when God said 'no.' In all of this I have seen God protecting singles from the wolf in sheep's clothing. The very elect was prevented from being deceived. Let God connect you with the right mate. Get God's approval. Don't always gravitate to the first person who comes on the scene promising you the world.

SMILE

There are people who have a knack for small talk by engaging others in lighthearted conversations. My husband can strike up a conversation with anyone, anywhere, and talk about any and everything. I'm not that outgoing. I can do it to a certain extent, then I run out of words. I want my light to shine, but at times struggle in opening up when I need to. I've asked God to help me in this area and He has. Les Brown, Motivational Speaker and Author, said, **"Your smile will give you a positive countenance that will make people feel comfortable around you."** A *smile* opens the door to allow the love and light of God to shine through you. I may run out of words, but I know how to give you a *smile*.

FRIENDSHIP

True friendship must be earned. When you are blessed with a friend in your life, that relationship must be proven. I think genuine friendships get messed up because we don't know the purpose of them. To be a friend you must be secure in yourself. You don't befriend someone to control them or for them to become you. If that's the case, you don't need to be a friend. Friends are confidants. They help and listen. They will make a way to be there for you. In the words of Samuel Taylor Coleridge, English Poet and Philosopher, – *"friendship is a sheltering tree."* What kind of friend are you?

HURT PEOPLE

People who hurt tend to hurt other people. They want others to feel their pain. Well my God, if the hurt ones keep on hurting, when will anyone ever get healed? To every person who is hurting and angry *STOP*. You may be angry at the world, but be it known to you today that God is not angry with you. This hurt and anger is killing you. God wants you to live. Suicide, sex, drugs and violence won't take the hurt away. Stop hurting the help He sends to you. When you fight the help, you're fighting God. I guarantee if you sincerely ask God right now to take the hurt and anger, He will do it. Oh God, rescue those who are calling on you. Deliver and heal in Jesus' name.

HURT LEADERS

Believe it or not, leaders hurt. Leaders have feelings. Leaders bleed. Leaders cry. We can hold them in high esteem, but remember they are made of flesh and blood like everybody else. If you are a leader in any capacity and are struggling with past or present hurts, get help. Believe it or not you are still *bleeding*. Your blood is contaminating others. I guarantee you that if you ask God to send you help for your personal issues He will. Don't get counsel from those you serve. Stop complaining to them. Stop trying to make them understand your plight. Get a trusted, seasoned leader or professional. When God connects you, don't reject it. Be open, truthful, honest, and unashamed. God never anointed you to lead by yourself!

LEADERS TREAT PEOPLE RIGHT

As a leader in any capacity, your first requirement is to respect people. We serve a relational God. He is *always* concerned about how we treat each other. You treat others as you want to be treated. I admonish every leader to watch how you treat those you are over. *Don't* minister to them from a place of hurt and bitterness. *Do not* lord over, beat down, or belittle God's people. If you lack people skills, get the necessary training and teaching. If you are impatient, lack self-control, are domineering, overbearing, unmerciful, harsh, etc. then *don't* lead. I don't care what your background is, who you served under, or what you came out of – *treat people right*. God allowed David to serve under King Saul. David learned what *not* to do as a king. You know right from wrong. The sheep aren't *always* as dumb as you suppose!

THE LESSON IN HURT

No one embarks on life's journey intentionally looking for hurt or offenses. We seek a life of peace and prosperity. Yet hurtful things happen. The reasons for hurt are too numerous to explore. The hurt can't be ignored – it really happened. Your hurt can be physical, emotional or psychological. Now, where do you want to go from here? God can heal you everywhere you hurt. He said what was meant for evil, He can turn it around for good. God knows how to capitalize off bad situations. I encourage you to renew your mind by considering this – *"forget what hurt you, but never forget what it taught you."* (Shannon L. Alder, Inspirational Author)

GETTING ALONG WITH PEOPLE

"The most important single ingredient in the formula of success is knowing how to get along with people." (Theodore Roosevelt, 26th President of the United States) This is a practical truth. You

really must take time and focus in on having a good relationship with people. We can be too quick to dismiss a person because of our narrow mindedness. We hear them but we don't hear them. We see them but we don't see them. Take time to really hear what they are saying. Take time to observe them. Observe with a positive perspective. There is some good in all of us. All personalities are not compatible but should always be respected. Ask God to give you wisdom about having good relationships with people. They could be the very ones God will use to bless your life.

RELATIONSHIP SPACE

I have noticed over the years that the best relationships are the ones that give me space. I'm talking about friendships and acquaintances. I'm a loner and an independent soul. Therefore, I'm not needy. Despite that, I value relationships. I know I can't live without them. Genuine and lasting relationships are developed over time. They are also trial and error. Sometimes daily interactions can be overwhelming – for example, moment by moment texting, hour by hour communications. We create unrealistic expectations and demands on each other. Relationships are healthier when there is space in them. This gives you time to develop yourself and allow God to perfect you. *"Nothing grows well without space and air."* (Patricia Monaghan, Poet and Writer)

CAN'T CHANGE OTHERS

We are living in an era of self-motivation, authenticity, being an original and not a copy, owning up to who we are, and so forth. This is good because it promotes self-worth. It breaks us from the strong influence of being what others want us to be. We say, *'be you!'* Yet on the flip side of all this self-worth we find ourselves still pressing people to be the way we want them to be. We want our children to talk like us. We want to whip our mates in line. We force our values on others who have not had our experiences. If God wanted us to be alike, He would have never given us different fingerprints. I will never be you. You will never be me. ***"Be not angry that you cannot make others as you wish them to be, since you cannot make yourself as you wish to be."*** (Thomas a' a Kempis, Christian Theologian and Author)

WORK YOUR OWN GROUND

The Bible teaches us to help those who are in need. Also, to help bear one another's burden. On the one hand we have an obligation to each other to a certain extent. On the other hand, we are not to be a crutch, but help you get up on your feet. Help is temporary, not permanent. Once we help each other, we are not to neglect ourselves and what we have been called to do. There comes a point in time that I can't do you and me at the same time. I've got to answer to God about me, not just you. So, I realize that I'm not envious of you or in competition with you. I've got to cultivate what I've been given to do. I don't want what you have, I only want my own. So, realize – ***"I'm too busy working on my own grass to notice if yours is greener."*** (Unknown)

DEFY THE ODDS

I am keenly aware of the fact that words can indeed hurt you. What people say about you, positive or negative, can have a bearing on your life. I don't think any of us grew up in an environment of only positive words because the world is so negative. If you find yourself being a product of the negative things people have said about you, it's time for you to have an audience with you and you. Look at yourself in the mirror. Say to yourself *"they all lied to me. I'm not what they said."* Release yourself from those words. ***"The greatest pleasure in life is doing what people say you cannot do."*** (Walter Bagehot, British Essayist and Journalist) Defy the odds.

MARITAL COMMUNICATION 1

Communication is a key factor in a marriage. It can build a relationship or tear it down. Words have power. How we use them can direct the course of a marriage. Men and women think different because God created them that way. In communicating to your mate, consider this: communication is verbal and nonverbal; listen for clarity and understanding, not just for your turn to talk; don't talk over each other; touch and talk; and give it your undivided attention.

MARITAL COMMUNICATION 2

Communication is a key factor in a marriage. Lack of communication opens the door to all sorts of misunderstandings, assumptions and disappointments. Consider the following in marital communication: give the *why* behind what you're saying; what you say should always build up and not tear down; your communication should be timely; designate dedicated time to discuss key matters of the marriage or family; don't let things build up; create an atmosphere where each partner can be open and honest without feeling penalized. Let's talk!

POWER OF SISTERHOOD

There is an authentic power in sisterhood. This power is something to be reckoned with when used in the right way. The power of sisterhood is derived from the experiences other women have lived through and they unselfishly grab hold of you to pull you through. This is genuine mental, emotional and spiritual strength. The power of sisterhood can protect as well. Only secure people protect. Let's make it safe for each other. ***"Sisters function as safety nets in a chaotic world simply by being there for each other."*** (Carol Saline, Journalist and Author)

SISTERHOOD – CONNECTED

A few years ago, the Lord connected me with a couple of women. One I knew a little, the other I didn't know at all. We would meet occasionally talking about ministry, our calling and a few personal things. We had ministry sessions with other women, but the three of us stuck together. We are secure in our own right, so there is no competition. I often questioned God regarding the purpose of the relationships. Not getting an answer, I went with the flow. Unbeknownst to me, these women met a need I had not realized – genuine friendship. These are not *"sisters by blood, but sisters by heart."* (Unknown) Thank you Lord for meeting a need I didn't know I had. The need to include others in my life.

SISTERHOOD – SUPPORT

I took on an endeavor that shocked my family and inner circle. It was something God said He would *allow* me to do. I don't get that too often! I explained it as a new assignment. The family figured I knew what I was doing and blessed me. The inner circle held their peace, looked at me and grunted, but never criticized. I never asked them how they really feel about it. Nevertheless, I pressed on to see what the end would be. The moral to this story is *"Support your friend, even if you don't support their situation."* (Unknown)

SISTERHOOD – BE THERE

In the interaction of sisterhood, women have the tendency to want to control each other. When a fellow sister takes steps of faith to walk out her destiny, it may not make sense. She doesn't always have time to explain her actions. *"Sometimes being a friend means mastering the art of timing. There is a time for silence. A time to let go and allow people to hurl themselves into their own destiny. And a time to prepare to pick up the pieces when it's all over."* (Octavia E. Butler, Science Fiction Author) Sisters, just be there.

SISTERHOOD – BE PROACTIVE

Everyone experiences rough times. Life comes at us hard with a series of unexpected circumstances. In the spirit of sisterhood, a bond is created whereby we have committed ourselves to each other. Trust has been earned. We have silently pledged allegiance to be available through thick and thin. So, our expectations from each other should be mature and proactive. *"When a friend is in trouble, don't annoy him by asking if there is anything you can do. Think up something appropriate and do it."* (E. W. Howe, Novelist and Editor)

SISTERHOOD – BE THANKFUL

I've learned to never take the people God sent my way for granted. They are in my life to push me into my destiny. No relationship is accidental whether it's good or bad. We always learn something from it. On many occasions God has sent people my way to challenge me – to provoke me – to light fires in me to move on. *"In everyone's life, at some time, our inner fire goes out. It is then burst into flame by an encounter with another human being. We should all be thankful for those people who rekindle the inner spirit."* (Albert Schweitzer, Theologian Writer and Philosopher) Take time to thank the ones who have lit your fire.

Perfecting SELF

LIFESTYLES

Life in Christ encompasses a new lifestyle. Lifestyles are not easily changed. We are creatures of habit. If the habit is good, we won't change it. We struggle with life in Christ because we want an immediate change for the better. Life in Christ begins with a new mindset. Do you realize how hard it is for you to change your mind especially when you've been convinced of something? Life in Christ is filled with new thoughts, new ways, and new methods. *"Your life does not get better by chance; it gets better by change."* (Jim Rohn, Entrepreneur and Author)

ACCEPT YOURSELF

"The unhappiest people in this world are those who care the most about what other people think." (C. JoyBell C., Author) Is that you? Are you so locked into the opinions of others that you have lost yourself? You must realize people have no heaven or hell to put you in. You were created to be different. You are going to be talked about whether you do good or bad. So how can you live free trying to please everybody? You can't. Free yourself from the opinions of others by accepting yourself and being content with you!

FORGIVE YOURSELF

Have you ever done something you have yet to forgive yourself of? You know – the regrets, should have, would have, if. You may have had experiences that were so bad you could not forgive yourself and are still hating yourself for it. Self-hatred sickens the body. Many auto-immune diseases such as lupus, Crohn's Disease, diabetes, rheumatoid arthritis, and multiple sclerosis have a spiritual root of self-hatred, self-bitterness, and guilt. These diseases cause the body to fight against itself. *"It's time to forgive yourself for that thing you keep beating yourself up about."* (Unknown) Be healed.

CHANGING ME

There was a time in my life where I believed I could change people and circumstances for the good. I felt like I had life's answers. I believed my way was the best way. Continuing on that path led to a lot of disappointments and frustrations. It left me with an attitude about any and everything. I wanted people to act right and be right. I put unrealistic demands on them. When they didn't meet my expectations, I wanted to cut them off. Who did I think I was with so many flaws of my own? God broke me down. He told me I was *not* the Holy Ghost and to get out of His business. Let me give you this advice from Victor Frankl, Australian Psychologist, – *"When we are no longer able to change a situation, we are challenged to change ourselves."*

EVIL THOUGHTS

Ephesians 6:12 says *"For we wrestle not against flesh and blood, but against principalities, against powers, against the rulers of the darkness of this world, against spiritual wickedness in high places."* These are spiritual forces that project diabolical thoughts and suggestions to your mind. They wage mental attacks.

Once you're convinced of their lies, they got you. *"It's hard to fight an enemy who has outposts in your head."* (Sally Kempton, Teacher of Meditation) Stop giving place to thoughts contrary to the Word of God. Wash your mind with God's Word. Believe it. Exchange negative thoughts with positive thoughts. Pull down those strongholds once and for all. (Second Corinthians 10:4)

ANGER

"Anger is never without reason, but seldom with a good one." (Benjamin Franklin, Former Speaker of the Pennsylvania House of Representatives) A fit of anger is like a balloon that pops right in your face. First, you have the balloon (that's you). Then you have a pump (something that ticks you off). Then you have hot air (you and the pump create this together – the pump sends the air your way, and you allow the air to build up inside you). If you don't do anything to diffuse the air – POP! You explode, frightening everyone in the immediate area. Nobody wants to see that. When you feel anger welling up inside you, strive to handle it constructively. If your anger is toward a person, talk things out. If it's just general anger, seek a calming place for yourself. Never forget that God is a very *present help* in the time of trouble. If your anger continues to get the best of you and it turns into rage, you need to consider some professional help. There is nothing wrong with that! It's still *help* from God.

RESOLUTIONS

Many people make New Year's *resolutions*. They start out with a positive outlook for the year. They *resolve* within themselves to accomplish certain things. What is a *resolution* anyhow? Before we can define *resolution,* we must define the word *resolute* which is taken from *resolution. Resolute* means to be determined, bold, not vacillating or shrinking. From *resolute* we get the word *resolve* which means to make up one's mind, decide firmly or cause to do. Then comes

101

resolution which means a thing *resolved* on, intention. In summary, *resolution, resolute, resolve* means to make up your mind on what you want to do and do it. No more lying to yourself. Do what you *resolved* to do. ***Be true to you!***

GOD'S YEAR

God has a way of revealing ourselves to ourselves. I'm sure by now you've said to yourself, and to others, that this is *your* year, season or time. You've also declared what's going to take place during this time since you have the power of life and death in your mouth. In speaking things into existence by decreeing and declaring, make sure it *all* lines up with the will of God. Your Heavenly Father would be so happy if you would let these upcoming times be His time and not *your* time. He already has plans for these times in your life. Give it to Him!

PERCEPTION

Your perception on life can make or break you. That perception is based on your experiences and its outcome. Don't allow your perceptions to limit you. There is more to life than experiences and outcomes. Life is a lesson learned. You will never have a life free of challenges and disappointments. Life will bring you things you don't like. ***"I will love the light for it shows me the way, yet I will endure the darkness because it shows me the stars."*** (Og Mandino, Author) Change your perception, change your life!

DISCOVERING YOU

How do you manage peer pressure? I'm talking about the pressure to perform according to other people's standards – a people pleaser. That can be good and bad. There's nothing wrong with pleasing our mates, family members, and others whom we love, admire and respect. I'm talking about the people-pleasing that causes you to be someone you're not. If that's the case, you have an identity crisis. You don't know who you are. *"Defining myself, as opposed to being defined by others, is one of the most difficult challenges I face."* (Carol Moseley Braun, Former United States Senator) Do yourself a favor and discover you!

PRIVATE PLACES

Each day as I live, I appreciate more and more how God created me. He created me from the inside out. What goes on inwardly is more important than what goes on outwardly. Take for instance your thoughts and attitude. People can say what they want, but no one really knows your thoughts. Thoughts are private. God allowed a place for thoughts to be sorted out privately. He also made a place for our attitudes to be hidden unless we decide to reveal them. Therefore, it's important to think before you speak or react. *The attitude within is more important than the circumstances without.*

AFFIRMING YOU

There are times where you must be your own encourager. No one can honestly affirm you the way you can. It's what you say to you that determines the outcome of your life. *"Have you reached that place in life where you enjoy your own company? Have you taken the time to enjoy your own personhood? When other people give affirmation, it reflects their opinion about you. When they leave, you may feel worthless and insignificant. But when you speak comfort and blessings to yourself, it reflects your own opinion about yourself. The best scenario is to enjoy both kinds of affirmation."* (T. D. Jakes, Pastor and Author)

ATTITUDE

One of the most significant decisions you can make on a day-to-day basis is your attitude about things. The attitude you choose either keeps you going or cripples your progress. It alone fuels your fire or assaults your hope. When your attitude is right there is no barrier too high, no valley too deep, no dream too extreme, and no challenge too great. Stop spending time fretting over things that can't be changed and give attention to the one thing that can be changed – your choice of attitude. (*Day by Day with Charles Swindoll,* Chuck Swindoll, Pastor and Author)

YOU ARE WHO YOU ARE

Too often we look to others to illuminate the person we are to be when we really need to look within ourselves. The Greater One is on the inside of us. Stop looking outside of yourself to define yourself! Not to say that other people don't and won't influence you. Just realize that at the core of your being, you are who you are. Just think how the elements of wind and water erode, smooth, and reshape even the greatest rocks. But from the beginning to the end, it's still a rock. Don't lose sight of you!

DON'T FORGET GOD

I know that as human beings we tend to think more highly of ourselves than we ought to. When you really think about it, your abilities and skills did not come from your own efforts. You are who you are by the grace of God. Never forget who empowered you to get wealth, skills, education, jobs, businesses, etc. It was never you, but it was how God created you. When you're feeling superior to everyone else, remember who created you and where you came from. *"And it shall be, if thou do at all forget the Lord thy God, and walk after other gods, and serve them, and worship them, I testify against you this day that ye shall surely perish.*" (Deuteronomy 8:19)

QUIET DOWN

When you are engaged in a heated discussion the more you raise your voice and act out, it tends to fuel the fire. You are hollering, they are hollering. This is the very place your adversary wants you to be. He wants you to act out and say whatever you feel. Then when it's all over he drops you like a hot potato leaving you feeling embarrassed and ashamed. If you have a quick temper and loose tongue, it's time to tame it with some self-control (temperance). Proverbs 15:1 says *"A gentle answer turns away wrath, but a harsh word stirs up anger."* Step out of your emotions, lower your voice, settle down, breathe and talk like you got some sense. Stop letting people take you where you don't need to be.

OFFENSES

Jesus tells us in His Word that offenses are going to come to us. (Luke 17:1) He also told us that He came to heal the broken-hearted and those who have been bruised. He specializes in healing broken hearts, offenses, misunderstandings, disappointments and anything else that has damaged your spirit. He came to make you whole – spirit, soul and body. It is not the Father's will for you to live wounded and hurt all your life. That's not who He created you to be. He wants you to be free and healed. Therefore, *"don't allow your wounds to transform you into someone you are not."* (Paulo Coelho, Brazilian Lyricist and Novelist) You are not your *wounds*.

Broken

Animal trainers break the spirit of an animal for it to be compliant. Horses are broken out of their wild nature and trained for usefulness. Some dogs are broken to comply with the owner's desires. Animals have a strong will that has to be brought into subjection to comply with man's needs. Not only is there a strong will in animals, but also in mankind. When you give your life to Christ, He then begins the process of breaking or conforming you by way of the Holy Spirit. This is to break you out of your wild and uncontrollable ways. ***"The sacrifices of God are a broken spirit; a broken and a contrite heart, O God, thou will not despise."*** (Psalm 51:17) You must be broken!

Stop

"Stop hating yourself for everything you aren't and start loving yourself for everything you already are." (Unknown) You *are* smart. You *are* a survivor. You *do* talk right. You *are* creative. You *do* have a relationship with God. You *know* how to pray, and God answers your prayers. You *are* friendly. You *do* have skills. You *know* how to budget. You *do* care. You *know* how to encourage others. You *can* read. You *can* comprehend. You *know* how to provide for your family. You *are not* lazy. You're *already* who God says you are. He's just perfecting those things that concern you. There's more that's right in you then wrong. Love yourself for everything you *already* are.

Self-Righteous

I have found myself struggling in situations I just didn't like. I didn't like the people, the environment, the location, etc. I'm talking about situations and places like my job, supervisor, co-worker, family, friends, etc. I almost despised it because I felt everybody, and everything was messed up. I was the only *right* one! I tolerated it but didn't like it. Then I made what I call an *'executive decision'* to come out of it. I decreed and declared my exodus. I constantly asked God to move on my behalf and nothing happened. I'm sure you have experienced the same thing — be honest! If this is you, let me help you. First of all, you are not as *righteous* as you think. Change your perspective. This is God's conforming work in your life. Embrace it. *"After you have suffered a while God Himself will make you perfect, stablish, strengthen and settle you."* (First Peter 5:10)

LEADERSHIP DETOX

To all the leaders and leaders to-be I want to encourage you to take time at various intervals of the year to detox your spirit, soul and body. Your work/ministry belongs to God. You are only a care-taker. Let your calling/assignment breathe. God can keep it if it's worth keeping. Get rid of the clutter within yourself. Release your soul from unhealthy relationships. Disconnect from toxic spirits. Confess to God what's going on with you personally because you are not exempt from self-examination and correction. Ask God to put someone in your life you can trust. Someone who will be honest with you about you. Get rid of blame-shifting. Own up to your stuff. Ask God to make you a *"better me"* so there will be a *"better we."* (Janae Fontaine, Minister)

GIVE OF YOURSELF

We are all familiar with the scripture that says, *"give and it shall be given unto you...."* (Luke 6:38) We quote this a lot at offering time in our local churches. But I want to take this *'giving'* into another direction. The *'giving'* I'm talking about is the giving of yourself. There is so much of you to give. Giving causes you to come out of yourself. Give wisdom from your life's experiences. Give a smile because God has smiled on you. Give a hug because you have the Comforter living in you. Give life because God has blessed you with another day. ***"We make a living by what we get; we make a life by what we give."*** (Winston Churchill, Former Prime Minister of the United Kingdom)

TRUTH LIBERATES

You've heard the saying *"be true to thyself."* In other words, stop lying to yourself and be truthful about you. Let's get honest within. You know what's right and wrong with you. You don't need anybody to tell you that. The problem is you think you're okay when you're not. Psalm 51:6 says ***"Behold thou desirest truth in the inward parts, and in the hidden part thou shall make me to know wisdom."*** God requires you to be true to yourself. Acknowledge what's going on with you. The truth in any form liberates. ***"If you tell the truth you don't have to remember anything."*** (Mark Twain, American Writer) Be free. Be truthful.

STANDARDS

"There are seven things that will destroy us: Wealth without work; Pleasure without conscience; Knowledge without character; Religion without sacrifice; Politics without principle; Science without humanity; Business without ethics." (Mahatma Gandhi, Indian Civil Rights Leader) Each of these traits come with a high price. This takes time and work. You only value what you work for. These traits are priceless. Each hard-earned trait defines your worth. Don't sell yourself cheap. Maintain the standards you worked hard to set.

REPUTATION

What is a *reputation*? *Reputation* is what's said or believed about a person's character. It is respectability. When people observe your life, what do they see? Better still, what is your character revealing about you? We all want to be known for something. Our lifestyles reflect who we are over a period of time and and defines us. Think about you – how you carry yourself, what you portray, what you want to be known as. *"Your reputation and integrity are every-thing. Follow through on what you say you're going to do. Your credibility can only be built over time, and it is built from the history of your words and actions."* (Maria Razumich-Zec, Corporate Entrepreneur)

REFLECTION

One of the disciplines God taught me is reflection on life. I'm a task-driven person. I get tunnel vision on whatever I must do. I tend to lose sight of everything else. That can produce an imbalance because too much of anything is not good. God balances me out. He stops me in my track. He causes me to take stock of what's around me amid what I'm doing. I used to think it was a distraction, but not so. It calms and settles me. It relaxes my body and soul so I can receive more from the Holy Spirit. I briefly reflect on where I was, look at where I am and keep moving forward with better clarity. I can complete the task with less stress.

Perfecting
SPIRITUAL DEVELOPMENT

STEPS

Psalm 37:23 says *"the steps of a good man are ordered by the Lord: and he delighteth in his way."* Steps represent a progressive process. A toddler's beginning steps teach him that his feet were made for walking. As the toddler grows his steps are more defined. He walks where he wants. He may experience liberty in walking but needs guidance because he's not fully aware of his surroundings and possible dangers. He begins to embark into territories he's never been in before. You're not a toddler, but there are some places in life you've never been before. Allow the Lord to order your steps and give you guidance. Steps are progressive. Slow your role. Take one step at a time. You will arrive at your destination.

GIFT OF REPENTANCE

Do you ever wonder why you keep going to God and asking forgiveness for the same offense or sin? Why is it so hard to get a grip on these issues in your life? Two things to consider in repentance. First, repentance is a command from God to everyone to repent.

(Acts 17:30) It's our first response to the lordship of Jesus Christ acknowledging His right to rule over us. Second, repentance is a gift from God enabling us to get back to Him. We then realize we not only hurt ourselves and others, but we offend God. You need God in every aspect of your life. Now is *not* the time to offend Him! Repent and mean it.

REPENTANCE DEFINED

Do you really repent when you ask God or others to forgive you? Repentance has to do with a change of mind. It means to go in another direction by not continuing down the same path of offense. The Hebrew meaning of *repentance* expresses an emotional stirring like difficulty in breathing while experiencing intense emotion. It involves our emotions in urging a change of behavior and character. It also implies a moral decision to turn back or make a radical change in attitude toward God and the sin or offense. What does repentance mean to you?

YOUR WORDS

The words you speak define you. How so you may ask? With your words you communicate your feelings, intensions and dislikes. God's words define Him when He says what He likes and dislikes, will and will not do, what He hates and loves. His words reflect His character. You know God by what He has said. Think for a moment about the words you speak. Are your words a true reflection of who you are? Are you accurately communicating your likes and dislikes, what you will and will not do, what you hate and what you love? Or are your words compromising – not reflecting your true characteristics? Be a person of your word. If you say it mean it. If you say it live it. If you say it, do it. If you say it, be it.

WORDS

Scriptures tell us that the power of life and death is in our mouth. (Proverbs 18:21) That power is the words we speak. Words are so powerful they create an atmosphere for good or bad. Due to the fact we do not take heed to our words, our present lives are a direct result of what we have said. We speak things we mean and don't mean. Regardless, we are blessed or snared by the words we have spoken. Your words express what you believe. Take time to listen to yourself. Listen to what's coming out of your mouth. You have the power to change your atmosphere and life by what you say and what you believe. How do you want it to be?

SPEAK WHAT YOU BELIEVE

Far too often we define ourselves by what we do and do not have. We tend to compare our lives with others – wanting what they have. Instead of always looking outward, we need to look within. All of mankind has a resident power – the power of his words. We speak what we believe – what we are convinced of. If you believe and are convinced that your present life will never change, it will remain that way. If your life is filled with drama, addictions, doubt, discouragement, despair, trouble on every hand, you can do something about it. You got the power in you to change it. Your life changes by what you believe and say. Change your mind – change your life. Change your words – change your life. You will have what you say!

THE POWER OF WORDS

The Bible tells us that God framed the world by the words He spoke. It also tells us that we are made in the same image and likeness as Him. Therefore, we have this ability to speak re-creative words. God placed such stock in His words that where He sends His word it will do what He said. (Isaiah 55:11) *"He sent His word and healed them.*" (Psalm 107:20) You have that same ability. What are your words doing when you speak? One minute we bless and the next minute we curse. What do you want your words to do? Are your words confused as to what they are sent to do? One minute you are healed and the next minute you are sick. One minute you are prosperous and the next minute you lack. Make up your mind. What's it going to be??

COST OF SALVATION

Witnessing and testifying about Christ to others is a glorious thing. We want people saved. It takes time to explain what salvation is all about. It's free, but it will cost you everything. Salvation requires allegiance to Christ which cuts into family and friendship ties. Matthew 10:34-39, MSG says *"Don't think I've come to make life cozy. I've come to cut – make a sharp knife-cut between son and father, daughter and mother, bride and mother-in-law – cut through these cozy domestic arrangements and free you for God. Well-meaning family members can be your worst enemies. If you prefer father or mother over me, you don't deserve me. If you prefer son or daughter over me, you don't deserve me. If you don't go all the way with me, through thick and thin, you don't deserve me. If your first concern is to look after yourself, you'll never find yourself. But if you forget about yourself and look to me, you'll find both yourself and me."*

COST OF DISCIPLESHIP

Count the cost before saying *yes* to Christ. This is your life, not an alternative lifestyle preferring to live like you want. Luke 14:26-27, MSG says *"Anyone who comes to me but refuses to let go of father, mother, spouse, children, brothers, sisters – yes, even one's own self – can't be my disciple. Anyone who won't shoulder his own cross and follow behind me can't be my disciple."* Then in verses 28-32 Jesus talks about counting the cost – thinking about what you're getting ready to do. You don't start building a house and not have what it takes to complete it. That's embarrassing. Or go into battle without considering the weapons you have in hand to win it. Verse 33 says *"Simply put, if you're not willing to take what is dearest to you, whether plans or people, and kiss it goodbye, you can't be my disciple."*

SPIRITUAL ALIGNMENT

When God created heaven and earth it was without form and void. Darkness was upon the face of the deep. God knew the earth had to come into alignment with what He wanted. Earth needed order and structure. The Spirit of God moved (hovered) upon the earth at the command of God. Just as God knew what the earth needed; He knows what you need. There are areas in your life that are without form, void and dark. You may need a spiritual alignment. Allow the Holy Spirit to move upon you – hover over you, be in you, and bring the light of God which reveals His order and structure.

APPOINTED LEADERS

I am so grateful for how Jesus set the Body of Christ in order. He gave us people He personally anointed and appointed to help lead and guide us on our spiritual journey. These individuals are not just limited to the five-fold ministry, but others who encourage, exhort and pray for our spiritual maturity. Hebrews 13:7, NLT says *"Remember your leaders who taught you the word of God. Think of all the good that has come from their lives and follow the example of their faith."* Look for ways to bless and honor your leaders. Thank them for the contributions they have made in your life.

LEADERS AND MEMBERS

Jesus saw to it that His people would be taken care of. When He left earth, He sent gifts of leadership to mature the Body of Christ. Leading people can be an imposing task. People don't like to be told what to do or how to do it. We have not been saved all our lives Living in the Kingdom of God is different from living in the world. Somebody must teach us the ways of Christ. Hebrews 13:17, NLT says *"Obey your spiritual leaders, and do what they say. Their work is to watch over your souls, and they are accountable to God. Give them reason to do this with joy and not with sorrow. That would certainly not be for your benefit."* Let's appreciate our leaders by obeying and not stressing them out!

GOD'S CHASTENING

In your walk with God have you ever realized He can be a little rough on you? That's because we can be some hard nuts to crack. God knows how to smooth us out. In Psalm 118 David talks about being in an adverse situation with his enemies. He needed God to step in and rescue him. God did just that. But during God's intervention, David said in verse 18 *"The Lord hath chastened me sore: but he hath not given me over unto death."* God chastened David during an adversity! The Message Bible says, *"God tested me, he pushed me hard, but he didn't hand me over to Death."* God will go to any length for us to walk in the authority He has bestowed upon us. Sometimes it takes a hard push from Him for us to realize what He placed in us to become it.

GOD HATES

When we talk to God, we tell Him what we like and dislike, what upsets us and how offended we are of other's actions. But when was the last time you considered what God likes and dislikes?

Proverbs 6:16-19, AMP spells it out: *"These six things the Lord hates, indeed, seven are an abomination to Him: A proud look [the spirit that makes one overestimate himself and underestimate others], a lying tongue, and hands that shed innocent blood, a heart that manufactures wicked thoughts and plans, feet that are swift in running to evil, a false witness who breathes out lies [even under oath], and he who sows discord among his brethren."* Let us so live as to not reflect what God hates!

GOD SAYS NO

People don't like to be told *no*. We want our way. Life has a way of teaching us that having our way all the time is not good. Let's consider God's reasons in telling us *no*. A while back I read a piece entitled *"God Says No."* (Claudia Minden Weisz, Poet) *"I asked God to take away my habit. God said NO. It is not for Me to take away, but for you to give up."* Well, so much for us consuming our prayer time asking God for something He's requiring us to do. Here's another one – *"I asked God to make my spirit grow. God said NO. You must grow on your own, but I will prune you to make you fruitful."* This helps you understand why you get cut back in the seasons of your life. God is making you fruitful. It's not the devil!

REVEALING ME

Have you ever had people in your life that really irritated you? I mean they really knew how to rub you the wrong way. I'm talking about the ones you avoid at all cost. The ones you must be prayed up for to interact with. For a while I thought I was under a curse or judgment from God because I always had to deal with difficult people. It was one right after another. After a while I began to realize that with each encounter it revealed a little bit more about me. Some I handled well, some not so well. God never removed them. He was making me, conforming me, renewing me. *"If you are irritated by every rub, how will your mirror be polished?"* (Jalal ad-Din Muhammad Rumi, Persian Poet)

STAND YOUR GROUND

God, more than anyone else, knows the tremendous magnitude of evil in the world. Evil comes to us all. It is no respect of persons. Yet, God keeps His people from evil. Jesus said in John 17:15 *"My prayer is not that you take them out of the world but that you protect them from the evil one."* God displays His power in us as we encounter evil on every hand. You are equipped to handle evil. *"Therefore, put on the full armor of God, so that when the <u>day of evil</u> comes, you may be able to stand your ground, and after you have done everything, to stand."* (Ephesians 6:13)

STAND

Your adversary wages a fierce and persistent battle against you to disbelieve God, give up, and walk away. He bombards your mind with everything he can for you to curse God and blame God for all your hardships. What is he up to? If he can get you to stop believing God, he's got you and your goods. He's nothing but a thief and a robber. He's trying to steal something from you. *"You are, at this moment, standing right in the middle of your own 'acres of diamonds.'"* (Earl Nightingale, American Radio Speaker and Author) *Stand* your ground. Don't be so easily moved.

HOW TO STAND

There is an opposing force in your life that wants to destroy your relationship with Christ. That force is the devil. So, how do you deal with him? One way is found in Ephesians 6:10-17. (1) Get your faith and trust up. Be strong in the Lord and in the power of

His might – His strength, not yours. (2) Know that your enemy is a spiritual enemy and not a physical one. (3) You need to protect yourself with the whole armor of God which is described in verses 14-17. (4) Having done all that is required of you – *stand*. What is the *all*? It's your life reflecting (showing evidence) of each part of the armor – truth, righteousness, peace, faith, salvation, and the Word of God. You *stand* in this and you will be a force to the devil that he cannot reckon with. *Stand*!

STAND FOR RIGHTEOUSNESS

Taking a *stand* for what you believe can be challenging when you want to do right by people. I mean calling a spade a spade when everyone else calls it a heart. Let me put it this way – being surrounded by wrong when you know you are right. It's when the majority says *yes,* and you say *no.* Ever been there? I've had to stand my ground for righteousness sake amid unrighteousness. I endured being ostracized – not liked. Yet in the end my *stand* proved to be right. ***"The enemies you make by taking a decided stand generally have more respect for you than the friends you make by being on the fence."*** (Henry Kissinger, Former United States Secretary of State) *Stand* for what you know is right. Remember you live with yourself and God.

DO ALL THEN STAND

Ephesians 6:13, NIV says ***"put on the full armor of God, so that when the day of evil comes, you may be able to stand your ground, and after you have done everything, to stand."*** I understand why I need the armor of God so I can be protected *when* the day of evil comes because it will come. The part I need to understand is ***"having done all or everything to stand."*** What's the *all* I need to do? Examine myself – make sure the adversary can't lay claim to anything in me such as un-forgiveness, bitterness, resentment, jealousy, sexual immorality, gossip, offenses, disobedience, murmuring/complaining, unbelief, doubt, ill-will in relationships, etc. If I don't repent, renounce and confess this stuff to God and man, then I have no right to expect the adversary to do anything I command. Have you done *all*?

SILENT STRENGTH

Michael Jordan, Basketball Player, once said, ***"My attitude is that if you push me towards something that you think is a weakness, then I will turn that perceived weakness into a strength."*** Are you up for the challenge to turn a perceived weakness into a strength? I think it's time for you to flip the script on your doubters/haters. Let them see how strong you really are. Allow God to demonstrate His strength in your weakness. The next time someone wants to argue with you, walk away. Don't say a word. Leave them to themselves. Don't give them the privilege of taking you where you don't want to go. Hold your peace because there is victory and maturity in *silence*.

LIARS

We talk a lot about what we don't like. Consider what God doesn't like? He detests sin on all levels. We tend to put sin in categories. One of the things God hates is lying. He hates a lying tongue, and a false witness that speaks lies. (Proverbs 6:16-19) He said in Revelations 21:8 ***"all liars shall have their part in the lake which burneth with fire and brimstone."*** Look at what happened to Ananias and Sapphira who lied to Peter about their money, but they lied to the Holy Ghost – instant death. (Acts 5:3) We don't think lying is a big deal. It's sin to God. When we consistently lie, we place ourselves in the enemy's camp whose leader is the Father of Lies – Satan.

POWER

A true born-again believer in Christ is one of the most powerful persons on the face of the earth. Why do I say that? *"As He is so are we in this world."* (First John 4:17) We are part of an elite group of people – God's royal priesthood, holy nation, peculiar people chosen (handpicked) by God. (First Peter 2:9) Our power comes from the indwelling of the Holy Spirit. The Holy Spirit is the power of God in the earth. There is no force on earth that can reckon with the Holy Spirit. Your body is the temple of the Holy Ghost which you have of God. (First Corinthians 6:19) Honor God in your body and in your life by maintaining a holy lifestyle. You represent the Kingdom of God. *"For the kingdom of God is not in word, but in power."* (First Corinthians 4:20)

GOD'S TIMING

I have been believing God to turn some things around in my life for a long time. I've kept the faith, decreed, and declared. I spoke to Him out of Psalm 31:2 – *"Bow down thine ear to me; deliver me speedily: be thou my strong rock, for a house of defence to save me."* I don't think He understood the word *speedily.* I think I died a hundred times waiting for Him to move. I know He heard me. (Proverbs 15:29) In the meantime, I learned to chill out. I came to David's conclusion in Psalm 31:15 when he said, *"My times are in thy hand."* God knows when to manifest your turn around. Keep the faith!

INFORMED

Our society is inundated with vast amounts of information. We pride ourselves in being well-informed, but we know nothing. I came across a couple of quotes that substantiates what I'm saying. *"Information is not knowledge."* (Albert Einstein, Theoretical

Physicist) ***"We are drowning in information but starved for knowledge."*** (John Naisbitt, Author and Public Speaker) *Information* is an accumulation of facts. *Knowledge* is what is known. You can inform me about investing money, but until I receive practical knowledge to actually invest, it means nothing. Every week you are informed about the ways of God. It will never change your life until you take information to knowledge then to application. Being informed about God and knowing God are two different things!

GOD'S TEACHING METHODS

I had some rough teachers when I was in school. One was a math teacher in junior high school. I dreaded going to that class. I really had to get myself together and concentrate on the math more so than on the teacher. Thank God she didn't call on me a lot. My first grade was a *"D"* or an *"F."* I think I passed with a low *"C."* What I learned was to pay attention to *what* she was teaching and not *who* she was. Winston Churchill, Former Prime Minister of the United Kingdom, said, ***"I am always ready to learn although I do not always like being taught."*** We want to learn new things from God, but God's teaching methods can prove to be discomforting. He knows how to teach us lessons we will never forget.

INNER CHALLENGES

Take a moment to look back over your life to see how many challenges you overcame. I know you thought you would die in the challenge, but you made it through. In the process of time, natural challenges will inevitably be met. It's the inward challenges that devastates us. ***"The battles that count aren't the ones for gold medals. The struggles within yourself – the invisible, inevitable battles inside all of us – that's where it's at."*** (Jesse Owens, African American Track and Field Athlete) Challenges have a way of revealing our true selves. Just remember, God is in the challenge with you.

It's His way of making you better. He said, *"after you have suffered a little while, will himself restore you and make you strong, firm and steadfast."* (First Peter 5:10)

PLAN OF ATTACK

Are you experiencing difficulties with adversarial forces? Is your binding and loosening ineffective? Are you seeing results from your decreeing and declaring? If not, you may need to read your manual again. Proverbs 20:18 says *"Make plans by seeking advice; if you wage war, obtain guidance."* Proverbs 24:6 says *"for waging war you need guidance, and for victory many advisers."* James 4:7 says *"submit yourselves then to God. Resist the devil and he will flee from you."* Come out of your emotions, anger and frustration. First get instructions and counsel from God as to how to handle your adversary. God knows him better than you do.

SUFFERING

No one wants to suffer. Human beings will always take the path of least resistance. Suffering is discomfort. Suffering is a part of life. Our suffering involves doing what we want versus what He wants. Perhaps a portion of First Peter 4:1-2, MSG can help ease some of the discomfort of suffering – *"Think of your suffering as a weaning from that old sinful habit of always expecting to get your own way. Then you'll be able to live out your days free to pursue what God wants instead of being tyrannized by what you want."* Nevertheless, *thy will be done*!!

SUFFERING IS DISCOMFORT

Suffering for the sake of Christ is very noble. That nobility costs you your life. Suffering is discomfort. Jesus said if you want to reign with Him you must suffer with Him. (Second Timothy 2:12) What does He mean by that? Jesus lived a life pleasing His Father. He overcame the discomforts of life to please the Father. To Jesus, life was nothing without the Father. Love for the Father helped Him to endure suffering. How much discomfort are you willing to endure to please your Heavenly Father? Examine your relationship with God. Are you pleasing more of yourself than pleasing God?

SERVING GOD

Serving God is more than a religious act. Serving God is more than knowing the Bible. Serving God has to do with a relationship. It's a relationship between a loving God and a sincerely grateful person. God extended His love to me while I was in a very ungrateful state. It was His love that drew me to Him. No one has impacted my life like God. Therefore, I am indebted to Him for the rest of my life. He has done more for me than I could ever imagine. So, there is no way I can be negligent in serving Him. I seek ways to serve Him better and He acknowledges it. Serve God with all your heart, your soul and mind. (Deuteronomy 6:5; 11:13)

GOD'S WORD WORKS

Isaiah 55:11 says *"So shall my word be that goeth forth out of my mouth: it shall not return unto me void, but it shall accomplish that which I please, and it shall prosper in the thing whereto I sent it."* When God speaks His Word to you, He expects it to do what He says. Therefore, you must listen and seek to gain an understanding of what He said. He expects to see His Word operating in your life. The seed of God's Word falls on the ground of your heart, but you must feed and fertilize it with faith and action.

PERSONAL PROPHECIES

I'm quite sure you've had God to speak to you prophetically. By prophetically, I'm talking about someone prophesying to you by the Spirit of God. Usually a prophetic word comes to you regarding something to take place in the future. Or it is a word describing where you are now and where God wants to take you. God sends the Word, but it's on you to position yourself for it to come to past.

PROPHETIC RESPONSE

When God speaks to you prophetically, He expects a response from you. You either agree or disagree, say *yes* or *no*, but respond. He may tell you something you didn't know about yourself or inform you of what His plan and purpose is for your life. No matter what He said, He needs to know you heard Him. Don't just walk away from a prophetic word from God without a responding back to Him. He's talking to you about your life. This is serious.

UNDERSTANDING PERSONAL PROPHECIES

I have been prophesied to on many occasions. Some things God spoke through His vessels were so overwhelming I could hardly contain it. The vessels spoke truth. I bore witness to it. It was meant to elevate my perception of what God was doing in my life. Much of it was for a specific time and season. I had to take heed. Then I had to begin aligning myself with what He said. And you should do the same.

GREATNESS OF GOD

Let's take a moment to reflect on the greatness of God. I mean taking time to consider His ways, methods and unconditional love.

Truly His ways are past finding out. God displays His greatness in the little areas of our lives by sending you a personal word of encouragement; meeting a need when no one knew; having people cross your path to take you to the next place in your life; showing you His strength in your time of weakness; saving and delivering a family member or dear friend. How great is our God!

PERSONAL SAVIOR

One of the things I love so much about God is how personable He is to each of us. I don't know how He does that. He can have intimate and personal relationships with each of us at the same time. I can't tell you the special ways God has manifested Himself to me. How He comforts me when I'm sad. How He identifies with what I'm experiencing. How He reminds me of His healing power when I get sick. How He encourages me when no one knows what I'm going through. He's my Personal Savior. Ralph Waldo Emerson, Essayist and Philosopher, put it this way – *"God enters by a private door into every individual."*

HE CARES FOR YOU

One year I attended a leadership conference that had a profound effect on my life. A pastor shared his personal testimony. It was so profound that it left us on our faces before the Lord. He ministered out of a broken place. He had been married and had children. He pastored a very prosperous church for 20+ years. He traveled all over the country ministering. Ministry became his god. As a result, his marriage ended in a divorce which really hurt his children. He turned the church over to another pastor. This left him in a broken place. He got through it and is back in ministry with a new perspective. He said, *"God cares more about the minister than the ministry."* Take heed!

STAY CONNECTED

Let me share this truth from Hebrews 10:25 – *"Not forsaking the assembling of ourselves together, as the manner of some is; but exhorting one another: and so much the more, as ye see the day approaching."* Why is it so important to physically go to church? First, there is strength in numbers. We are spirit. Our spirits connect when we are in each other's presence. Don't think for a minute that habitual doses of online, e-church or bedside Baptist is going to cut it. Sometimes you just need to be *"in the room"* (Vikki Johnson, Author and Speaker) to receive that corporate anointing. You can see it and hear it, but experiencing it is priceless. Not only that, your adversary knows how to cleverly keep you out of touch with fellow saints. T. D. Jakes, Pastor and Author, said, *"the trick of the enemy is isolation before destruction."* Let's go to church!

HEARING GOD

God left nothing to chance when He saved us. He even saw to it that we can hear Him amid chaos and confusion. That's where the Holy Spirit steps in. He enables us to hear what the Father is saying to us at any given moment. Therefore, it is so important to be filled with the Holy Spirit. *"Whenever the Holy Ghost speaks, He testifies that He has been in the boardroom of Heaven. Hearing from Him causes us to lift our head. Just when satan thought he had you, to his amazement you begin to shout. He doesn't know it, but you heard a word."* (T. D. Jakes, Pastor and Author)

IN THE WILL OF GOD

Just because you are in the will of God does not mean you won't encounter adversities and ill-treatment. The will of God includes challenges to our faith. Billy Joe Daugherty, Pastor and Author, testified in his book *"Knocked Down, But Not Out."* – *"Now storms and hits will come in life, but just because you have some challenges doesn't mean you're not in the will of God. I've rejoiced in that thought many times in my life, and particularly during the most recent altercation when I was punched in the eye during an altar call."*

GOD WANTS MORE

Your walk with Christ is to be progressive. You should be advancing. That's why God requires more from you. The longer you walk with Him, the more He expects from you. God gives you a timeframe to deal with the things you procrastinate on. Time is precious. It waits for no one. You don't have as much time as you think to surrender to Him, change your ways, believe Him to a greater extent, etc. He's expecting more from you because He has proven Himself to you repeatedly. Show Him more!

MAINTAIN YOUR DELIVERANCE

I can't tell you how many times Christ has set me free. Yes, I was freed from a life of sin when I accepted Jesus as my Savior. Then I found I had to deal with the tendencies of sin in my life. The tendency to lie, backbite, not forgive, stay angry, cheat, etc. was still there. You know what I'm talking about! As the Holy Spirit convicted and delivered me from those ungodly habits, I had to maintain my deliverance. Jesus told the woman caught in adultery – *"go and sin no more."* (John 8:11) She had a responsibility to stay free. *"Maintain what you have obtained."* (Richard Scott, Bishop and Teacher)

SIGNS OF A BELIEVER

You are a respected person when you say what you mean and mean what you say. People respect your standards because you demonstrate what you say. Well, we call ourselves believers, but do we really believe? Do our lives reflect belief in Christ? Is there any evidence that you are a believer in Christ? Mark 16:17 says **"And these signs shall follow them that believe...."** What signs follow you that demonstrates you're a believer in Christ? Instead of talking it, we must be it. You may believe Christ, but are you demonstrating Christ?

THREE WEEKS

God knows how to break us out of old habits. He will allow things to come that break up our routine. He's always up to something new, fresh and different. Don't expect to stay the same. He breaks old habits to incorporate new ones. It takes 21 days to break a habit – three weeks. If you stick with God's Word for you – His plan, His counsel – you stand a good chance of being more like Him in three weeks – going from glory to glory and faith to faith.

KEEP AT IT

I'm sure you have started many endeavors such as exercise, losing weight, saving money, cleaning out your closet, etc. My goddaughter began a path of physically improving her body. After weeks of working out and curbing her food intake, she hopped on the scale for her weekly weigh-in. To her dismay there had been no change. She got a little discouraged but began to encourage herself. She remembered being taught *faithfulness*. Being faithful is remaining consistent even when you don't see the results. Don't be driven by what you see. Just remember, you may not always see the change immediately, but something is happening. Consistency produces lasting results.

DISCIPLESHIP

During my early years in Christ, the bulk of the teachings were on being a disciple of Christ. The emphasis was being Christ-like and disciplined in His ways. Somehow discipleship lost its popularity in the church. I don't understand why since we say we are Christians. Discipleship is discipline. We must be disciplined to the teachings of Christ. If you are going to follow His discipline you are going to have to carry your own cross. (Luke 9:23) The cross represents crucifixion. Some old worldly/fleshly ways are going to have to die – deny yourself. (Matthew 16:24) You just can't live like you want and be a disciple of Christ.

FEAR OF GOD

Proverbs 9:10, NIV says *"The fear of the Lord is the beginning of wisdom and knowledge of the Holy One is understanding."* The word *fear* here means reverence, respect, and homage. It does not mean to be afraid of. We talk a lot about having the fear of the Lord back into the church and back into people's lives. Our world is filled with so much disrespect and dishonor that we have contaminated the house of God - contaminated our personal relationship with Him. Don't allow the ways of the world to distort your reverence and respect for God. He is all-knowing, all-powerful. Nothing escapes Him. He is God and besides Him there is no other.

PURE HEART

Proverbs 4:23 says *"Keep thy heart with all diligence; for out of it are the issues of life."* The New International Version says, *"Above all else, guard your heart, for it is the wellspring of life."* Your heart reveals what's in you. What's in your heart is revealed in what you say. See to it that you keep your heart pure by filling it with the Word of God and good/positive things. Allow the Holy Spirit to reveal good and wholesome things to you from the Word of God and from life's experiences.

GOD SEES

Proverbs 15:3 says *"The eyes of the Lord are in every place, beholding the evil and the good."* I want you to remember this scripture when you want to take matters into your own hands, get revenge or even want something bad to happen to someone. God not only *sees* everything, but He *knows* everything. The wicked will be taken care of. Let Him deal with them. Just make sure you are right – doing good, acting right by living a life pleasing to Him. He's looking at you as well.

RESTORATION IN THE WORD

Every time I read God's Word, I become awe struck at the power and revelation it brings. The Bible is just as fresh today as it was when it was first pinned thousands of years ago. Let's just take the scripture in Psalm 119:93, NLT – *"I will never forget your commandments, for you have used them to restore my joy and health."* God's Word restores your joy and health. A God-breathed Word has the power to bring joy back into your life when there is despair all around you. It has the power to restore your health – to touch your body. I dare you to believe and take the Word as it was given. You just might experience some genuine joy – some restorative healing.

INFORMED NOT TRANSFORMED

Modern technology is fast and quick. We are a well-informed people. Information on any subject is obtained with the click of a button. We are overwhelmed with so much information to the point we aren't taking time to fully process it. The mind can only comprehend so much at a given time. I've gathered information on a certain matter, used it for what I needed, and thought about it no more. I was just informed. This Bible you read, and quote is not meant for you to be merely informed. It's meant for you to be changed, enlightened and renewed in your mind. Your Bible is not for information but for transformation.

TRANSFORMATION

When God chose you to be saved and you acknowledged His call, it wasn't just for you to escape some type of catastrophe in your life at that time. He *saved you to change you* back into His image and likeness – change the way you live and think. Therefore, the encounters and experiences you have are meant to produce a godly life. That's why it says in Romans 12:2, NLT – ***"Don't copy the behavior and customs of this world, but let God transform you into a new person by changing the way you think. Then you will learn to know God's will for you, which is good and pleasing and perfect."*** A changed mind will produce a changed life.

YOUR MIND

While growing up I had little control over the negative things I heard. There was always cussing, fussing and fighting in my household. To this very day I've wondered why I never cussed and fought like my family. I had inward anger, but never physically fought or engaged in unnecessary arguments. I kept a lot to myself believing no one really wanted to hear what I had to say anyway. I immersed myself in magazines picturing beautiful homes, and successful/professional people wearing nice clothes. My mind was set. I set out to make my own life. God turned that mindset into something good by allowing me motivate others to live better. ***"You are who you are and what you are because of what has gone into your mind. You*** *can change who you are and what you are by changing what goes into your mind.* " (Zig Ziglar, Author and Motivational Speaker)

CONSISTENCY

I want to give you a formula for positive consistency in your life. In the words of Mahatma Gandhi, Indian Civil Rights Leader, – *"Keep your thoughts positive because your thoughts become your words. Keep your words positive because your words become your behavior. Keep your behavior positive because your behavior becomes your habits. Keep your habits positive because your habits become your values. Keep your values positive because your values become your destiny."*

HERE I AM

There's a lyric to a song that says *"Here I am to worship. Here I am to bow down. Here I am to say that you're my God."* (Israel Houghton, Singer and Songwriter) When was the last time you told God *"here I am for You?"* Not asking anything but presenting yourself to God as a living sacrifice. This is a place of surrender – a place of humbling yourself to your God. *"Here I am"* implies *"Lord I'm not hiding anything. I'm naked and bare before You."* To get to a place like this you must acknowledge your own frailties and realize without God you are nothing. All that you are is because of Him. This is the place of transformation where God is waiting for you.

GROWTH

Second Peter 3:18 says *"But grow in grace and in the knowledge of our Lord and Saviour Jesus Christ."* Key words in this scripture are *grow - grace - knowledge.* (1) *Grow* – growth is progressive and not stagnate. How much have you grown in Christ? When you grow you change. (2) *Grace* – this is God's empowerment in your life. It is His ability in you. It is a favor you did not deserve. But you have to grow in it. (3) *Knowledge* – your knowledge of Christ must increase. How much more of His Word, way and will do you know and understand? There must be progressive growth, greater trust in His grace, and increased knowledge of Him. Let's grow!

SUBMIT TO GOD

I have stated repeatedly that in and of ourselves we are no match for the onslaught of the devil. The battles are spiritual. We need the power of the Holy Spirit to deal with them. For every war waged against you, you need a different strategy. You can't always use the same method to counterattack your adversary. The Holy Spirit will give you the right strategy to manage him. James 4:7 says *"Submit yourselves therefore to God. Resist the devil, and he will flee from you."* Before you go off into your tantrum, settle down and submit yourself to God. Ask Him how to handle the situation. He has ways you know not of. You may have to be quiet, worship, speak the word, etc. But first *submit*! Then the devil will flee. That's God's order.

HE'S COMING BACK

I want to remind you that Christ is coming back. Will you be ready? Is your relationship with Christ intact? Are you really saved, or should I say born-again? Are you hot, cold or lukewarm in your relationship with Him? Are you faking it or really living a Christ-like life? Can you say with a surety that your name is written in the Lamb's Book of Life? You say you know Christ, but does Christ know you? Revelation 22:12 says *"Behold, I am coming soon, and I shall bring My wages and rewards with Me, to repay and render to each one just what his own actions and his own work merit."* Examine yourself to see if you are in the faith. You don't have as long as you think.

TRIED AND TRUE RELATIONSHIP

In Genesis 22 God puts Abraham's relationship with Him to the test. God wanted to see where Abraham's heart was in serving Him. You know the story. God promised Abraham a son. He gave him one in his old age. Abraham knew the promise God gave him would produce a multitude of people through his blood line. God made good on the promise. God wanted to see if Abraham was only serving Him because of a fulfilled promise. God asked Abraham to sacrifice his son – put the promise on an altar. Abraham proved his allegiance through obedience. While getting ready to sacrifice his son, God stopped Abraham and said, ***"Now I know that you fear God because you have not withheld from me your son, your only son."*** (Verse 12) Could you give up your long-awaited promise if God asked for it?

TIMES OF REFRESHING

We all need a time of refreshing. A natural refreshing revitalizes the soul. A spiritual refreshing revitalizes the spirit. How do you get a spiritual refreshing? Acts 3:19 says ***"Repent ye therefore, and be converted, that your sins may be blotted out, when the times of refreshing shall come from the presence of the Lord."*** *Repent* here means to change your mind, focus and direction. Change your perspective. *Be converted* means don't use old materials, old ways. When you change your perspective (repent), and embrace new ways, you become *refreshed*. But you only get this in the *presence* of the Lord. Spend time with God about *you*!

WEDDING PREPARATION

I attended the wedding of a dear friend of mine. I remember when she told me she was engaged. We were super excited. Then she told me about the preparations she was making for the wedding.

She and her fiancé had planned to pursue other streams of income to finance the wedding. It took her out of her comfort zone but paid off in the end. As a result, they had long workdays. They experienced tiredness along the way. As the wedding date approached, they had reached their goal. The wedding was beautiful and so was the honeymoon. You are espoused to be the bride of Christ. What preparations are you making to insure a successful wedding?

GOD'S EXPECTATION

Quite often we are challenged to raise our level of expectation in God. Increasing our expectation means increasing our faith because we know without faith it is impossible to please Him. What is God expecting from you? What is He requiring of you? The answer can be summed up in three words – *growth, progress* and *obedience*. You are a living being created by God. He is expecting you to grow. Anything living must grow. He is expecting to see progress in what He has endowed you with. That progress involves obedience. Don't disappoint Him!

GOD'S CONFIDENCE IN YOU

Hebrews 10:35 tells us not to *"cast away our confidence"* in God because it will pay off. We know that to be true. What about God's confidence in us? He's confident we will make it through the challenges of life. How do we know that? He has prayed that our *"faith fails not."* (Luke 22:32) God is confident that we will walk with Him all the days of our lives. How do we know that? *"For it is God who works in you to will and to act according to his good purpose."* (Philippians 2:13) God is confident you will never lose sight of Him. How do you know that? He said, *"lo I am with you always even unto the end of the world."* (Matthew 28:20) Don't let Him down!

Don't Go Back

Galatians 5:1 says *"Stand fast therefore in the liberty where-with Christ hath made us free and be not entangled again with the yoke of bondage."* God went to great lengths to secure your freedom. You were in spiritual bondage, yet He created you to be spiritually free. That spiritual freedom was forfeited because of Adam's sin of disobedience. Sin did not stop God from loving you. God so loved the world that He gave His only begotten Son to bring you back into fellowship with Him. (John 3:16) Your spiritual liberty cost God His son. It cost His son his life. The least you can do is not go back into the bondage of sin.

Stand Fast

Galatians 5:1 says *"Stand fast therefore in the liberty where-with Christ hath made us free and be not entangled again with the yoke of bondage."* To *stand fast* means to hold your ground. Hold your ground in the liberty and freedom Christ provided for you. Fight for your liberty. Fight to stay free from the bondages of life. Guard and protect your spiritual liberty. Don't let anyone take away the liberty you have in Christ. Christ gave His life to guarantee that liberty. The least you can do is hold on to it for it is your life.

Spiritual Maintenance

How do you maintain your spiritual freedom in Christ? The latter part of Galatians 5:1 says *"be not entangled again with the yoke of bondage."* A yoke is used to steady and control movement. A yoke is used to guide and keep you going in a certain direction. Before you came to Christ you were yoked with sin. Christ took that yoke off you. Now you are yoked with Him. Matthew 11:29-30 says *"Take my yoke upon you and learn of me; for I am meek and lowly in heart: and ye shall find rest unto your souls. For my yoke is easy, and my burden is light."* You maintain spiritual freedom by taking on His yoke – allowing Him to lead and guide you in the path of spiritual liberty.

SELF-EXAMINATION

When was the last time you examined and/or evaluated your life in Christ? Hopefully you have seen quite a bit of progress. You've come a long way. Don't be too hard on yourself. God is still working on you. Are you okay with the progress that's been made? Of course, all of us can be better. Celebrate the progress. Stay yielded to more change. *A change in behavior begins with a change in the heart.* He's standing at the door of your heart waiting to come in at every interval of life. He's got something good for you – it's called *change!*

CHANGE

It's a glorious thing to celebrate the wonderful changes that have taken place in your life. Changes that have made you a better person. No one can appreciate that like you can. We can get so caught up in our own change that we want everyone else to change like us. We impose our personal changes on others, only to discover they don't want it. You know – a parent gets saved and immediately wants the rest of the family to line up with this new life. Not happening! *You can't change people, that's God's job. Just keep working on changing yourself. Actions speaks louder than words!*

CONSIDER YOUR WAYS

In the first chapter of Haggai God had an aught against His people. They were to rebuild His temple. It remained an unfinished project for 16 years. The people kept saying it *'wasn't time to rebuild.'* God answered through the prophet Haggai and said, *"**Is it a time** *for you yourselves to be living in your paneled houses, while this house remains in a ruin?"* Then He said, *"consider your ways."* The New International Version says, *"give careful thought to your ways."* How many times have you neglected the needs of your local church while ensuring your needs were met first? It's like giving God leftovers. I am a witness that if you take care of God's business first, He will take care of yours. You owe Him – *"Consider your ways."*

EMPOWERMENT EVENTS 1

Local fellowships and various ministry groups have annual conferences, revivals and retreats for us to be enlightened, inspired and motivated. Emphasis is placed on topics that enhance our spiritual growth. Speakers come from far and near. Excitement and anticipation fill our hearts. We prepare ourselves physically, financially and spiritually. Everyone wants a move of God. We seek a change like never before. The Word is delivered. Hearts were made glad as God showed up and showed out. Now what? *"You get the spark, but you put it in park!"* (Janae Fontaine, Minister)

EMPOWERMENT EVENTS 2

Conferences, revivals, workshops and retreats are designed to motivate and inspire you. Special messengers are selected to bring forth a Word from the Lord. They are specialists in their own way. God sends divine revelation and instructions. The Holy Spirit moves to validate the Word with signs and wonders following. What a rush! What a hype! What a move! It was exactly what was needed to get you moving. God did His part. What are you going to do? Don't let this be another *"unction with no function!"* (Theresa Scott, Author and Teacher)

Perfecting
THANKS

THANKSGIVING DEFINED

In one of my study bibles I came across a definition for *thanksgiving*. It said, ***"a public acknowledgement or celebration of God's goodness."*** Thanksgiving has to do with what God did and does for us just because He wants to. Truth be told, God blesses us despite ourselves. We take a lot of things in life for granted. We live as though the world owes us something. We think we should automatically benefit from a good deed. Let's come out of ourselves – realize if it had not been for the Lord on our side, where would we be. Take a moment. Thank God for undeserved blessings!

THANKS

In this age of entitlement being thankful is a rarity. People think the world, the government, and others owe them something. You were created and put on this earth to give of yourself. Giving is the spice of life. Giving brings inner satisfaction that has no monetary value. Being thankful is a response to someone who has given to you. If you *really* want to be in the will of God give thanks. First Thessalonians 5:16 says ***"Be joyful always; pray continually; give thanks in all circumstances, for this is God's will for you in Christ***

Jesus." Give thanks *in* all things – not *for* all things. There's always something to be thankful for even in bad situations. Give thanks!

THANKSGIVING

In the season of thanksgiving, I want you to pick out seven days. In those seven days purposefully give thanks to God. Find something to be thankful for. Meditate on it and genuinely thank God for it. Then take it to the next level. Think of someone you are thankful for. Make it a point to communicate that to them. Don't just tell God you're thankful for them, tell them. God has placed some good people in your life. Don't take them for granted – be thankful.

Perfecting TRUST

TRUST DEFINED

What is *trust*? *Trust* is confident expectation. *Trust* is a firm belief in the reliability of a person or thing. There are two sides of the coin of *trust*. One side is you. Can you be trusted? Do you fulfill people's confident expectation in you? Are you reliable? Can you be counted on to do what you say? The other side of the coin is God. Can God be trusted? Does He make good on your confident expectation of Him? Is God reliable? Can He be counted on to do what He said He will do? You will only trust what has been proven to you. Your side of the coin of trust needs to be polished so it can reflect your trustworthiness.

TRUST GOD

Proverbs 3:5 says ***"Trust in the Lord with all thine heart; and lean not unto thine own understanding."*** The Message Bible says, ***"Trust God from the bottom of your heart; don't try to figure out everything on your own."*** We quote this scripture yet fail to do it. *Trust* is confident expectation. This is not trust in man, but trust in God. I always say trust must be earned. Truly God has earned a place of trust in your life after all He has done for you. He has never wronged you. You may not have liked His methods, but He has always had your welfare in mind. Trust Him to give you the right wisdom, strategies and timing for everything in your life. When you don't understand, He does. Allow Him to enlighten you about life. You gave Him your life, now trust Him with it!

VALUE OF TRUTH

It's amazing how we can be so easily turned away from the truth of God's Word especially when we have experienced it. What kind of power can someone have over you to move you away from the Word and goodness of God? I may not have understood everything God did in my life, but I do know it was all for my good. God has never wronged me. He has never lied to me. He allowed every experience to make me better. I may not have liked His methods, but He knew what was best. ***"O foolish people of God, who hath bewitched you, that you should not obey the truth?"*** (Galatians 3:1)

ABOUT THE AUTHOR

Dr. Theresa Scott, a Christ follower and disciple for more than 40 years, is an author, teacher and empowerment speaker. She is the mother of two children, five grandchildren and one great grandchild. She ministers with her husband, Apostle Dr. Richard Scott, at Grow in Grace Worship Center, Delmar, Maryland. (www.gigwc. com)

Dr. Scott received her Doctor of Divinity degree from Spirit of Truth Institute, Richmond, VA; Master of Christian Education and Bachelor of Biblical Studies degrees from H. E. Wood Bible Institute & Theological Seminary, Alexandria, VA.

Dr. Scott comes with a wealth of experience and wisdom in walking with God. She is a sought-out speaker for workshops, conferences and intimate settings. Her passion is for people to accept themselves and walk in the power of their individuality.

She was the President of Humble Time International Women's School of Ministry empowering women to raise their standard of living. Later she aired her radio broadcast – *Perfecting Moments* – empowering God's kingdom one minute at a time in the Maryland area. She has also hosted *Tea Time with Dr. Theresa Scott;* sacred sisterhood events where real-life issues were addressed featuring women with expertise in all aspects of life. Her current journey is authoring books to leave a legacy in the earth.

*"I keep asking that the God of our Lord Jesus Christ, the glorious Father, may give you the Spirit of wisdom and revelation, so that you may **know him better**."*

(Eph. 1:17, NIV)

For Speaking Engagements, Media Interviews, Social Media and Other Inquiries
Dr. Theresa Scott
P. O. Box 2083
Salisbury, MD 21802
Email: lgcebks@gmail.com
Facebook: Theresa Scott
Instagram: Dr. Theresa Scott

www.ingramcontent.com/pod-product-compliance
Lightning Source LLC
Chambersburg PA
CBHW071803090426
42737CB00012B/1923